FORJANDO PATRIA

FORJANDO PATRIA

PRO-NACIONALISMO

(FORGING A NATION)

BY

Manuel Gamio

TRANSLATED AND WITH AN INTRODUCTION BY

Fernando Armstrong-Fumero

UNIVERSITY PRESS OF COLORADO

Published by the University Press of Colorado
1580 North Logan Street, Suite 660
PMB 39883
Denver, Colorado 80203-1942

Originally published as *Forjando Patria (Pro Nacionalismo) por Manuel Gamio*, © Libreria de Porrúa Hermanos, México, 1916

The University Press of Colorado is a proud member of Association of University Presses.

The University Press of Colorado is a cooperative publishing enterprise supported, in part, by Adams State University, Colorado School of Mines, Colorado State University, Fort Lewis College, Metropolitan State University of Denver, University of Alaska Fairbanks, University of Colorado, University of Denver, University of Northern Colorado, University of Wyoming, Utah State University, and Western Colorado University.

ISBN: 978-0-87081-966-7 (hardcover)
ISBN: 978-1-64642-858-8 (paperback)
ISBN: 978-1-60732-041-8 (ebook)

Library of Congress Cataloging-in-Publication Data

Gamio, Manuel, 1883–1960.
  [Forjando patria. English]
  Forjando patria : pro-nacionalismo / by Manuel Gamio ; translated and with an introduction by Fernando Armstrong-Fumero.
       p. cm.
  Includes bibliographical references and index.
  ISBN 978-0-87081-966-7 (hardcover : alk. paper) — ISBN 978-1-64642-858-8 (paperback) — ISBN 978-1-60732-041-8 (ebook) 1. Mexico—Civilization. 2. Mexico—Politics and government—1910–1946. I. Armstrong-Fumero, Fernando. II. Title.
  F1234.G1713 2010
  972—dc22
                                                                                              2009045465

Cover illustrations: *Caballero Aquila* (Eagle Knight), illustration from 1916 edition of *Forjando Patria* (*front, top*); 1924 photograph of Manuel Gamio, Library of Congress call number LC-F8-29998 (*front, bottom*).

To my students

Contents

Illustrations

Preface

Why *Forjando Patria*? Why Now?

I was motivated to translate *Forjando Patria* by the memory of a seemingly endless series of miscommunications and tensions that marked my earliest discussions with Mexican colleagues. This was an experience that I shared with many of my contemporaries as we all began doctoral research in different regions of the world. We all entered "the field" with knowledge of the anthropological traditions of the global south that was based entirely on the relatively few texts that were available in the United States or on secondary sources. This translation is an attempt to give Anglophone readers access to a particular set of topics that have been mentioned extensively in secondary literature but that are rarely discussed with a nuanced sense of their original context or of the many textual ambiguities that can lend themselves to different interpretations. It is a gesture toward cultivating a more linguistically and culturally democratic sense of the history of the social sciences, which can contribute to more meaningful transnational dialogues with colleagues trained in different national traditions.

The need for more translations of primary source material was made clear to me through some specific points of disagreement and confusion that emerged consistently in my first discussions with Mexican colleagues. Early on, I learned that many books by Mexican scholars that I considered to be "classics" actually contained fairly particular interpretations of the national reality. It also seemed that I read many of these books grossly out of context. A number of my Mexican colleagues pointed out that having one's work translated into English often transformed a fairly idiosyncratic author into a speaker for the national tradition at large. In other cases, I was gently rebuked for my assertion that texts like Fernando Ortiz's *Cuban Counterpoint* (1995 [1940]) or José Vasconcelos's *La Raza Cósmica* (1979 [1926]) were examples of the "undisciplined" literary genre that gave rise to discussions of *mestizaje* and national identity in Latin America (see Trigo 2004). Although the essayistic traditions that these texts embody are cherished by Latin American scholars, the treatment of this genre as *the* authentic form of regional expression involves an erasure of the "disciplined" social science literature that has been written in Spanish by university-trained anthropologists since the 1910s and 1920s.

One tendency in Anglo-American studies of Latin America that has been particularly contentious in my discussions with Mexican colleagues is the use of theoretical writings from South Asian postcolonial studies as analogs for postcoloniality in the global south as a whole.[1] There is much truth to the observation that, whatever their national origins, scholars from former British colonies enjoyed a certain privilege in writing in the English language. It is largely because they are readily accessible in the language of international academic prestige that these texts have enjoyed a circulation far beyond their original national context. Even if the major themes in many of their discussions were anticipated by generations of Latin American scholars who debated over the nature of postcolonial identities and non-European modernities, many key Spanish-language texts are inaccessible to any but area specialists and native scholars.

In sharing these anecdotes, I do not mean to critique works written by my colleagues back home in the United States. In defense of contemporary scholarship in Latin Americanist cultural studies, I would argue that certain kinds of interplay between "disciplined" and "undisciplined" narrative registers *did* play an early and decisive role in defining the national trajectory of "disciplined" social sciences like anthropology in Mexico. Likewise, I recognize that my own training and thinking have been influenced powerfully, and for the better, by English-language traditions of postcolonial scholarship. Even so, the contentions that marked so many of my discussions with my Mexican colleagues have made me conscious of a series of linguistic and disciplinary prejudices that simply cannot be ignored.

In the end, the frictions that I encountered owe as much to the training of graduate and undergraduate students as they do to any fundamental incompatibility between different national traditions. It goes without saying that courses

....

[1] For a discussion of this problem by a noted anthropologist, see Lomnitz 1999.

on the history of anthropology in the United States tend to focus on the development, decline, and transformation of a series of "great" theoretical traditions rooted in European and North American academies. When students encounter national anthropological traditions from the south, it is almost always through secondary sources. Just as there are a number of English-language studies that have discussed Mexico's native tradition of anthropology (Bernal 1980; Hewitt de Alcántara 1983; Tenorio Trillo 1999; Lomnitz 2001), others have outlined the development of "national" ethnological and archaeological traditions ranging from Peru (de la Cadena 2004) to Japan (Ivy 1995), Egypt (Mitchell 2002), and Israel (Zerubavel 1995). In these insightful critiques, the roots of national anthropologies are presented in a fundamentally critical tone, most often as examples of "traditional" social sciences that were complicit in different projects of colonialism or state formation. This is also prevalent in the relatively few texts by more contemporary Mexican and Latin American authors that have been translated into English, which tend to be critiques of "traditional anthropology" and nationalism (Bartra 1992; Bonfil Batalla 1996; García Canclini 1995). When Anglophone students read critical analyses of histories of these national traditions through the filter of secondary sources, they cannot "revisit" foundational texts as they might do with Malinowski or Boas. In the worst cases, this trains students to evaluate contemporary political and theoretical agendas against a caricatured—and unread—tradition from the global south.

In this sense, this translation of *Forjando Patria* is meant to defamiliarize the well-trodden fields of revolutionary nationalism and national anthropologies for both Mexicanists and scholars working in other geographical areas. For students of Mexico and Latin America, the sheer scope of the topics upon which Gamio touched, his integration of theoretical principles with accounts of contemporary events, and his negotiation of foreign and national intellectual traditions provide an especially rich portrait of a complex and often misunderstood moment of intellectual history. For more general readers, the epistemological and political quandaries of "native ethnographers" will be seen through the lens of a distinct national inflection and a crucial historical moment. In *Forjando Patria*, Gamio contemplates the colonial heritage of Mexico after nearly a century of independence and in the midst of a revolutionary struggle that would transform the political life of the nation. The Mexican Revolution of 1910, the fundamental backdrop for *Forjando Patria*, was among the first of the great national revolutions of the twentieth century. It brought about an early and unique configuration of radical and liberal ideologies, modernizing schemes, and divergent class interests that would play out again and again, in different forms and in other national contexts, over the course of the century. In this sense, students and researchers studying other parts of the world will find a distinct national perspective and configuration of a series of experiences that have parallels in other postcolonial settings.

Besides my debt to the late author, I am grateful to a number of colleagues whose encouragement and input were essential in completing this translation. First, I thank John Weeks for valuable advice on how to produce a translation that would be useful to contemporary scholars. I am also grateful to Angel Roque, Jocelyn Chua, Elliot Fratkin, Suzanne Gottschang, Donald Joralemon, Ruchi Chaturvedi, and Joannah Whitney, all of whom gave me valuable feedback on the introduction or other aspects of the text.

Fernando Armstrong-Fumero

FORJANDO PATRIA

Manuel Gamio and *Forjando Patria:* Anthropology in Times of Revolution

In 1909 and 1926, Manuel Gamio made two crucial trips from Mexico to the United States. In the first, he arrived as a student at Franz Boas's Department of Anthropology at Columbia, making him the first Mexican to obtain an advanced professional degree in anthropology from a foreign university. In 1926, he returned to the United States as an exile, fearing for his life in a tense climate of internal struggles that marked the years after the 1910 Mexican Revolution that ended the long dictatorship of Porfirio Díaz. The period between these two trips across the Rio Bravo was crucial for Gamio and for the history of modern Mexico. In that stretch of time, Gamio completed first a master's degree and later a doctorate at Columbia University and collaborated with foreign scholars in conducting research in his home country. He also aligned himself with the military faction that was currently consolidating its power through a series of new political institutions and a vibrant nationalist ideology, creating a strong new state that would be governed by over seventy years of single-party rule. With this combination of academic credentials earned abroad and commitments to revolutionary projects at home, Gamio helped to found the precursors of anthropological and archaeological institutions that would play a crucial role in Mexican cultural and development policies throughout the twentieth century. His relationship to North American academics, revolutionary state formation, and the study of ancient and contemporary societies makes his life and work a useful point of entry for understanding the particular valence that anthropology would take in twentieth-century Mexico.

Published in 1916, *Forjando Patria* marks the midpoint of the crucial period in Gamio's career that was bounded by his studies at Columbia and his eventual exile. In this text, he outlined a professionalized anthropology that would serve as a "science of good governance" for the emergent revolutionary state. It is a broad-reaching manifesto in which the author seeks to reconcile the anthropology that he had learned at Columbia University with nineteenth-century narratives about modernization and even older anxieties about the nature of postcolonial national identity. Many of the recurrent themes of this text had appeared in the works of Mexican scholars since the nineteenth century (see Molina Enriquez 1909; Sierra Mendez 1969 [1902]; Hale 1989; Shadle 1994; Saez Pueyo 2001). But what makes *Forjando Patria* exceptional is the fact that it was written and read amidst the emergence of revolutionary institutions that would define political life for three quarters of a century, and that can still be perceived amidst more recent reconfigurations of Mexican democracy and nationalism.

A. GAMIO, BOAS, AND ANTHROPOLOGY BETWEEN THE PORFIRIATO AND REVOLUTION

Gamio's own youth and early intellectual formation bridge the distinct realities of Porfirian and revolutionary Mexico, something that is quite evident in the major themes explored in *Forjando Patria*. Born in 1883, he grew to adulthood in the period of peace and relative economic progress often referred to as the *pax porfiriana*. This was a time when the strong, centralized dictatorship consolidated by Díaz brought a three-decade respite from the instability that had governed during the first two thirds of the nineteenth century. Born into a reasonably prosperous family, Gamio completed his preparatory studies at the Escuela Nacional Preparatoria (National Preparatory School), an intellectual bastion of the positivism that was the official philosophy of Porfirian Mexico. A cocktail of Comte and Spencer, Mexican positivism was a moderate, or even conservative, inflection on a tradition of liberal thought with roots in the early nineteenth century. Stressing a positive knowledge of national realities over the blind application of European democratic principles on an insufficiently "civilized" populace, the positivist doctrine of "evolution over revolution" was perfectly suited for a period marked by a strengthening of technocratic rule and strict limitations on traditional democratic institutions (see Zea 1953; Hale 1989; Saez Pueyo 2001).

Gamio's biographers have seen other incidents in his early life as signs of an emergent "revolutionary" consciousness. After completing his preparatory studies, he briefly studied engineering before leaving school to take over the management of a failing family farm. There, observing the conditions of the local workers, he developed the admiration for Mexico's indigenous peoples and the desire to improve their living conditions that were to influence his later career (see Gonzalez Gamio 1987). This particular anecdote resonates with the genre of narratives that was at the core of post-revolutionary nationalism in Mexico. In popular histories and grade-school texts, the biography of the "revolutionary" tends to hinge on a pivotal encounter with the suffering of the poor and downtrodden and the subsequent development of a social consciousness attuned to cross-class sympathies. Such solidarity between members of the mestizo middle class and the indigenous population is also a recurring theme in *Forjando Patria*.

It was in the last year of the Porfirian dictatorship that Gamio had his first encounters with anthropology, through courses taught at Mexico's National Museum of Anthropology. During this time, it is evident that he had relatively little influence in the Mexican intellectual scene. His earliest attempts to conduct independent archaeological investigations were frustrated by Leopoldo Batres, the irascible National Inspector of Monuments. Batres was a favorite court intellectual of President Díaz and notoriously jealous of other researchers.

As doors closed to him at home, Gamio turned to members of an expatriate community with important academic connections in the United States. On the recommendation of the Anglo-American antiquarian Zelia Nuttal, who had had her own nasty conflicts with Batres,[1] he was admitted into Franz Boas's anthropology department at Columbia University. Gamio was completing his master's degree in New York when the first shots of the revolution were fired, and he returned home in 1911 to what would be more than a decade of almost continuous warfare (Gonzalez Gamio 1987; de la Peña 1996: 44–46).

....

[1] Batres is well-known for conflicts with foreign and Mexican archaeologists. Zelia Nuttal, whose *tertulias* in Coayacán were frequented by Gamio and other archaeologists (see Tozzer 1933), had a conflict with Batres regarding the discovery of a ruin on Isla de Sacrificios, Vera Cruz. In her discussion of this incident, she lists additional conflicts of "the Batres-Sierra coalition" with foreigners the Duc de Lobat and Alfred Maudslay and Mexicans "Señor del Paso y Troncoso and Señor Francisco Rodriguez (both quondam directors of the National Museum), Dr. Nicolas Leon, Señores Manuel Gamio and Ramón Mena and many others deserving of every consideration and encouragement" (1910: 280).

Research by foreign scholars continued in Mexico despite the reigning climate of instability, and Gamio was integrated into the Escuela Internacional de Arqueología y Etnología Americana (International School of American Archaeology and Ethnology). The International School was maintained through support from the national governments of the United States, France, Mexico, and Prussia and from the private universities of Pennsylvania, Columbia, and Harvard. It opened its doors in 1911 and closed just four years later under political pressure from warring revolutionary factions (see de la Peña 1996: 58–62). During the brief period of its operation, the International School hosted European and Anglo-American archaeologists and ethnologists, including Boas, Alfred Tozzer, George Engerrand, and Eduard Seler. In a time when Mexican philosophers and artists were seeking alternatives to the hegemonic positivism of the Porfiriato, the instructors at this institution offered novel theoretical currents that would influence some of the most important post-revolutionary scholars (Gonzalez Gamio 1987; de la Peña 1996; Matos Moctezuma 1998: 79–80).

Gamio's primary research as a fellow of the International School was in archaeology. Much of this consisted of ceramic surface collections and test pits that would later be recognized as the first systematic applications of stratigraphic excavation methods anywhere in the world (see de la Peña 1996; Bernal 1980). This work also led to Gamio's designation as Mexico's Inspector General of Monuments, a post that had been dutifully abandoned by his old nemesis, Leopoldo Batres, when Díaz was ousted from the presidency (Matos Moctezuma 1998: 62). This represented a general changing of the guard in the Mexican academy, as Porfirian intellectuals found themselves marginalized after the loss of their old political patrons. In the chapter of *Forjando Patria* titled "Our Intellectual Culture," Gamio makes a triumphant reference to the fall of these "sackcloth pontiffs" (see Chapter 21).

If the development of anthropology in Europe and the United States is associated with Indian agents, explorers, and university professors (see Patterson 2001), the "creation stories" of Mexican anthropology and cultural policy often focus on how revolutionary intellectuals like Gamio consolidated new political and educational institutions amidst this climate of instability and political transition. Popular historical and literary treatments have represented the politically engaged man of letters as a member of the petit bourgeoisie who sought the sponsorship of a military or political leader after the collapse of traditional academic institutions (see Krauz 1999; Lomnitz 2001; Rama 1996; Zea 1945). As the foreign members of the International School fled Mexico,

Gamio's political and professional survival became even more contingent on his ability to cement patronage from one of the political factions currently vying for power.

It was in this context that *Forjando Patria*, a broad manifesto for a nationalist cultural project, served as a crucial work of political positioning and intellectual diffusion (de la Peña 1996: 61). Many of the essays published in 1916 as *Forjando Patria* had originally appeared in Mexico City newspapers, and most of them are written in a clearly middlebrow register that appealed to educated laypersons. In them, Gamio moved beyond his earlier focus on archaeology to comment on the importance of socio-cultural anthropology and other contemporary themes ranging from art and literature to national industry and gender relations. Throughout the text, anthropology is presented as a science that should be sponsored by the state and that constituted an essential body of knowledge for the success of revolutionary reforms. As he noted:

> It is a given that anthropology, in its true and amplest conception, should be the basic form of knowledge for good government. Through anthropology, one gains awareness of the population that is the source of both rulers and those who are ruled over. Through anthropology, one can characterize the abstract and physical nature of men and peoples and deduce the appropriate methods to facilitate their normal evolutionary development. (p. 32)

Gamio's incorporation into the revolutionary state took place a year after the publication of *Forjando Patria*, through an office created for him in Venustiano Carranza's administration as head of a newly created Departamento de Antropología (Department of Anthropology). He remained in this post after Carranza was overthrown in 1920 by the members of the Sonoran Dynasty (Álvaro Obregón, Plutarco Elias Calles, and Adolfo de la Huerta). Gamio's political survival after the Sonoran coup may have been because of the high regard that new president Álvaro Obregón had for his work. Obregón is known to have read *Forjando Patria*, a book that he referred to as a "profoundly scientific study of the true origins of our national ills" (in Gonzalez Gamio 1987: 47).

Both Carranza and the Sonorans formed part of what later Marxist historians characterized as the bourgeois wing of the Mexican Revolution (see Córdova 1979a, 1979b; Semo 1979). Natives of northern states of the republic from social backgrounds roughly comparable to Gamio's, these leaders shared interests and political programs quite distinct from those espoused by the peasant armies of Francisco Villa and Emiliano Zapata. This political orientation is clearly reflected in *Forjando Patria*, particularly in Gamio's discussion of Zapata's peasant movement, which was engaged in all-out war with the Carranza faction by 1916 (see Chapter 34, "Three Nationalist Problems"; see also Womack 1969). As a promoter of the rights of Mexico's indigenous people, Gamio argued that there was a kernel of legitimate "indigenism" at the core of Zapatismo. However, he also argued that it was necessary to isolate this from two of the movement's other signature aspects: "banditry" and the manipulation of ignorant masses by "reactionary" holdovers from the old regime (see pp. 158–159). Gamio further noted that "Zapatismo is a localist and temporary denomination that is bound to disappear, whereas Indianism has persisted vigorously in Mexico since Cortés placed his standard on the sands of Villa Rica" (p. 158). In effect, this statement implies that the only salvageable elements of the Morelos peasant movement were those that could be co-opted into paternalist state institutions. After the final defeat of Zapata and Villa, this means of incorporating dissent and transforming subaltern groups into corporate constituencies of the state became a signature feature of postrevolutionary Mexican politics (see esp. Córdova 1979b).

The presidency of Álvaro Obregón marked the height of Gamio's direct influence on state-sponsored institutions. In the second year of Obregón's presidency, he and a team of researchers published the monumental *La Población del Valle de Teotihuacán* (1922). This multivolume study combined a general census of a regional population from central Mexico with a discussion of the local archaeological record, physical types, folkloric traditions, and economy. This was intended to be the first of a series of studies (each to be executed over the course of one or two years) focusing on populations exemplifying each of the republic's "regional cultures" and its various "urban cultures" (Gamio 1922: xi). This ambitious project had received official support from the president, and an English translation of the report was accepted with high honors as Gamio's doctoral dissertation at Columbia University (de la Peña 1996: 62).

Gamio's political fortunes took a marked turn for the worse during the presidency of Obregón's successor, Plutarco Elias Calles (1924), when his role in exposing a series of misappropriations within the Secretaría de Educación Pública (Secretariat of Public Education or SEP) greatly compromised his political position.[2] Threats on his life sent him into exile in the United States in 1925 (see Gonzalez Gamio 1987), where he researched and wrote two well-

---

2   The Department of Anthropology was transferred to the SEP, and Gamio was promoted to Undersecretary of Education in 1924 (de la Peña 1996: 62).

known studies of Mexican migration (1930, 1931). Although these texts fall somewhat beyond the scope of this introduction, I should note that they are broadly consistent with Gamio's assumptions about the transmission of "modern" forms of culture and are currently being reexamined by historians as an important document of the politics of emigration and especially *return* migration in early twentieth-century Mexico (Walsh 2004).

Gamio himself returned to Mexico after several years, when the former president Calles was cast into political disgrace. Although he served in a number of additional government posts, he played a more prominent role in international organizations and research than in the centralized archaeological and indigenist institutions—most notably the Instituto Nacional de Antropología e Historia (National Institute for Anthropology and History or INAH) and the Instituto Nacional Indigenista (National Indigenist Institute or INI)—that were founded in the 1940s (Gonzalez Gamio 1987; Bernal 1980). Headed by later figures such as Alfonso Caso Andrade and Gonzalo Aguirre Beltrán, these centralized federal institutions defined policy toward indigenous ethnic groups and archaeological heritage for the half century to come. The INAH and INI were staffed primarily by alumni of Mexican universities, where anthropology curricula generally revolved around a model of applied research and national cultural policy similar to that proposed in *Forjando Patria*.

Although these institutions enjoyed a great deal of continuity over the decades that followed, the fate of this nationalist anthropology was closely tied to the legitimacy of the revolutionary state. A series of challenges to heritage and indigenist institutions and the assimilationist model of applied anthropology became one of the defining experiences of Mexican scholars trained since the late 1960s. I will return to these critiques in the last section of this introduction.

If we read *Forjando Patria* retrospectively we can see a series of themes that largely defined the disciplinary identity, institutional framework, and internal debates of Mexican anthropology and that conditioned its divergence from a neighboring tradition in the United States. In this sense, the most significant aspect of the text is Gamio's characterization of the discipline as an applied social science that would help the revolutionary state to create a unified, healthy, and progressive national society. This emphasis marks an early point of divergence from the Anglo-American tradition in which Gamio received his early training (see Tenorio Trillo 1999). Although Franz Boas and many of his North American students also wrote at length regarding the relevance of anthropology for governmental institutions (see Patterson 2001), the political and social contexts that figured in Gamio's early career made the state an almost inevitable source of sponsorship.

The realities of revolutionary Mexico also influenced the theoretical content of Gamio's writing. A century of postcolonial anxieties about national identity and a deep-seated liberal tradition made Boas's strict cultural relativism less viable for Gamio and generated a series of tensions that are at the heart of *Forjando Patria*. In the following sections, I will look at some of the specific ways in which Gamio used this text to adapt what he had learned at Columbia to the heritage of nineteenth-century liberalism and the exigencies of revolutionary politics. As I will argue, some of the tensions and compromises that appear in this text reemerged in the work of later scholars and institutions and contributed to the particular valence of anthropology in modern Mexico.

B. ARCHAEOLOGY: A SCIENTIFIC AND MONUMENTAL PAST

Before 1916, Gamio's primary contributions to anthropology in Mexico had been as an archaeologist. As I mentioned earlier, he is widely credited with the first successful application of the stratigraphic excavation that became a fundamental method for modern archaeology (Gamio 1909, 1917, 1924; see also Bernal 1980). In *Forjando Patria*, he placed these technical innovations at the core of a nationalist archaeology that was distinct from both the amateur antiquarian studies of the nineteenth century and the research-focused tradition that was concurrently emerging in the United States. For Gamio, this new archaeology had a dual purpose: to understand how indigenous societies lived in the past and to promote national unity in the present.

In *Forjando Patria*, Gamio defined archaeology as "the study of the culture or civilization of the human groups that inhabited our country before the Conquest" (p. 71). The deep historical roots that he posits for the essence of Mexican nationhood are evident in his frequent references to diverse indigenous groups as "Mexicans"—and not just "Aztecs" or "Maya." This extension of "national" history into the distant past is consistent with the appropriation of pre-Hispanic civilizations that had been a central feature of Mexican nationalism since the last years of the colonial period (Keen 1971; Brading 1973; García Canclini 1995; Tenorio Trillo 1995; Lomnitz 2001) and that has analogs in many other "national" traditions of archaeology (Zerubavel 1995). State-sponsored archaeology in Mexico historically has placed great emphasis on the didactic use of pre-Hispanic remains, something that is evident in styles of restoration and museum display that stress monumentality and juxtapositions of modern art and ancient artifact that are rarely seen in the United States (Braun 1993; Florescano 1993; García Canclini 1995; Castañeda 1996; Rodríguez Garcia 1997; Errington 1998). Many foreign scholars, especially those who are fresh from experiencing the tricky terrain of securing permits from state-operated heritage institutions, point to nationalistic interpretations and uses of the pre-Hispanic past as marks of the fundamentally nonscientific criteria that govern Mexican archaeology.

What often appears as a lack of objectivity to foreign scholars is, in fact, a tension that archaeologists trained in Mexico have negotiated or struggled with for decades (see Armillas 1987; Matos Moctezuma 1979; Rodríguez Garcia 1997; Vasquez León 2003). The roots of this ambivalent interplay among science, technical stewardship, and monumentalism are already evident in *Forjando Patria*. However, writing in the 1910s, Gamio seems not to have perceived any disjuncture between rigorous excavation and nationalist celebration. In fact, the essays on archaeology in *Forjando Patria* promote an almost seamless integration of the scientific study of archaeological materials and a deeply subjective means of "experiencing" the pre-Hispanic past.

Even in 1916, *Forjando Patria* was received by a readership that was familiar with a rich body of historical writings on the native cultures of Mexico and with "indigenist" themes in art and literature (Keen 1971; Cifuentes 2002). But for Gamio, these more traditional genres of writing stood in a subservient position to the kinds of incontrovertible artifactual evidence that could be generated by modern archaeology. He argued, for example, that the profusion of names that the colonial authors used to refer to the natives of the Valley of Mexico should be reduced to the three broad cultural horizons that he had identified in his own stratigraphic excavations at several sites: Archaic, Teotihuacan, and Aztec (p. 40; see also Gamio 1909, 1917, 1924). But even as Gamio participated in the formulation of a body of methods that would set standards for technical rigor for archaeologists around the globe, the ultimate goal that he posited in *Forjando Patria* was to transform this objective knowledge into a deeply emotional experience for members of the general public. This objective is particularly evident in his assertion that a rigorous knowledge of the past could help people experience "authentic" aesthetic reactions to pre-Hispanic art (see Chapter 10, "The Concept of Pre-Hispanic Art") and how it might inform the creation of specialized settings in which students could "live with" pre-Hispanic and colonial ancestors (see Chapter 15, "The Values of History").

This vision of a nationalist archaeology was enshrined by heritage organizations such as the INAH. Decades later, Mexican archaeologists who became interested in different theoretical interpretations of the rise of ancient civilizations found themselves to be marginalized within institutions that held dogmatic views about the nature of pre-Hispanic history and the goals of excavation and restoration (see Armillas 1987). By the 1960s, the divergent political and intellectual project first posited in *Forjando Patria* contributed to a growing gap between what some Mexican anthropologists derisively referred to as the "monumental restoration school" and a "New Archaeology" then popular in the United States. This gap figures into a larger disciplinary crisis that I will discuss in more detail later.

C. CULTURE, EVOLUTION, AND *MESTIZAJE*

Whereas discussions of archaeology reflect the empirical studies that Gamio had conducted by the time that he wrote *Forjando Patria*, most of the other chapters in the text deal in a more theoretical fashion with the culture of contemporary Mexico. The rigorous scientific definition of culture is a recurrent theme in these chapters, and it is one of the aspects of the book that most clearly reflects the tensions and intersections between revolutionary nation building and foreign strains of social science. Like his mentor Franz Boas, Gamio espoused a broadly relativistic definition of culture, treating cultural particularities as the result of long-term environmental influences on a given society. At the same time, his work involved the markedly non-relativistic assumption that national progress hinged on the assimilation of indigenous people into a homogeneous Hispanic culture. Slippage between non-relativistic and relativistic definitions of culture reflects ambiguities that were common in the work of Boas and many of his North American students until the 1930s and 1940s.[3] In Gamio's case, it was also conditioned by the evolutionist heritage of Mexican

....

[3] Historian of anthropology George Stocking has pointed out that Boas often slipped into humanist concepts of culture that characterized culture in qualitative terms or as a degree of intellectual attainment, and only formalized a relativistic definition around the 1930s under pressure from his own students (Stocking 1966: esp. 870–871). In this context, some of the hierarchization that Gamio used between "national" and "indigenous" culture is not a misreading of an already relativist social science so much as the product of a generalized ambiguity in the discipline's terminology in the 1910s and 1920s. It is useful, for example, to compare the ambiguous and ambivalent relationships that Gamio establishes among culture, civilization, material progress, and nationality with Edward Sapir's well-known essay "Culture, Genuine and Spurious" (1924).

positivism and by the emphasis on modernization and national unity that was central to revolutionary-era political rhetoric.

The most clearly relativistic discussion of culture in *Forjando Patria* is in Chapter 22, "The Concept of Culture." There, Gamio counters accusations that Mexicans are an "uncultured" people with the argument that

> [m]odern anthropology has established the fact that culture is the conjunction of all of the material and intellectual features that characterize human groups. It does not attempt to establish grades regarding cultural superiority nor to anachronistically characterize peoples as cultured or uncultured. Culture is developed by the collective minds of peoples; it emerges from their historical antecedents and from the environment and circumstances that surround them. That is to say, each people has the culture that is inherent to its ethnico-social nature and the physical and biological conditions of the ground that they inhabit. It is not sensible for any people to think of its *cultura* or *Kultur* or culture as superior to those of others, or try to impose it by force. (pp. 103–104)

In other cases, Gamio uses "culture" more or less interchangeably with "civilization" and seems to establish clear hierarchies between indigenous and European types. In Chapter 21, "Our Intellectual Culture," he noted that

> [n]aturally, however brilliant and surprisingly developed pre-Hispanic civilization was for its time, the traces of it that we see today seem anachronistic, inappropriate, and impractical. There are indigenes who have a surprising knowledge of the course of the sun, the moon, and other celestial bodies. In pre-Columbian times, these individuals would have been respected astrologer-priests. But now, they would seem ridiculous if they were installed in an astronomical observatory. Indian herbalists that possess the secret of a vast medicinal pharmacopeia would have justly been considered medical notables in the past, but our modern doctor disdains them and accuses them of being untrained poisoners. (pp. 97–98)

Differences in the semantic role played by culture in different chapters of *Forjando Patria* might be read as Gamio catering to the "folk" definitions of his nonspecialist readers. However, there is a degree of consistency in the tensions between relativistic and non-relativistic uses of the term. Although Gamio argued for the equal validity of all cultural expressions when considered *as such*, he makes numerous references to a tendency toward "scientific progress" as the characteristic that ultimately marked the superiority of European civilization. Gamio says little about *why* such knowledge was less evident among the pre-Hispanic civilizations of America, but he seems to consider this to be a qualitative difference between European and indigenous cultures that made the conquest of Mexico into a foregone conclusion (see especially Chapter 30, "Spain and the Spanish").

Even if there appears to be an evolutionary hierarchy between indigenous and "modern" culture in *Forjando Patria*, it is not quite the same hierarchy that was imagined by the Victorian evolutionists and many Porfirian positivists. For Gamio, the pinnacle of Mexican evolution would not be a carbon copy of the most "civilized" nations of Europe but the development of a mixed or intermediate culture that was better suited to its times and its environment than either the European or indigenous. There are numerous uses of the term "evolutionary" in reference to the cultural fusion that accompanied the biological admixture of *mestizaje*. Gamio refers to the "evolutionary incorporation" of European and Indian art in Chapter 11 ("Art and Science in the Period of Independence") and to the "evolutionary cultural fusion" that took place during the colonial period in Chapter 34 ("Three Nationalist Problems"). He characterizes this latter phenomenon as taking place when

> Indians gradually adopt new manifestations of culture by appropriating them to their own nature and necessities, or when they transform those of their own civilization by emptying them into new molds. In this case, fusion takes place with the wise intuition that comes with spontaneous evolution.
> (p. 159)

This idea of evolutionary fusion figured prominently in Gamio's assertion that native crafts and aesthetics that developed over three centuries of colonial rule were better suited to national realities than more prestigious forms imported from Europe by the independent republic (Chapter 21, "Our Intellectual Culture"; Chapter 11, "Art and Science in the Period of Independence"). This favorable contrast of colonial to "exotic" arts is also extended to industry and political systems. Gamio argues, for example, that artisan traditions that emerged between the sixteenth and eighteenth centuries could be developed into a national industry that was better suited to the aptitudes and consumption patterns of most Mexicans than were many imported foreign technologies (see Chapter 28, "Our National Industry"). Likewise, he suggested that laws implemented by the colonial viceroys were more sensitive to the necessities of the indigenous population than republican laws that were modeled on European societies (see Chapter 16, "Revision of the Latin American Constitutions").

Some aspects of this argument are consistent with the older positivist tradition, which argued that Mexican society needed to modernize through a gradual evolutionary process rather than through "metaphysical" political principles transplanted blindly from Europe (see Zea 1953; Hale 1989). Still, there is a marked contrast between Gamio's praise of colonial legislation and the positivist tendency to characterize that period of national history as being dominated by irrational "theological" thought. Furthermore, Gamio extended his critique of "exotic" legislation to the Reform Constitution of 1857, an almost sacred document for most positivists (see Hale 1989).

This critique of some of the most cherished liberal traditions of the nineteenth century implies a relativistic analysis of law and government. It is an acknowledgment that legal principles that persons of "European civilization" would consider to be universal are, in fact, conditioned by the culture and historical experience of parts of the world that are very different from Mexico. Besides the influence of Boas's relativism, this argument reflects critiques of the nineteenth-century liberalization of land tenure and other key economic sectors that became more permissible within the populist ideology of the revolution. Carranza and the Sonorans, for example, cultivated a new kind of mass politics through which the bourgeois state generated consent among the largely indigenous peasantry by reinventing forms of collective land tenure that had been undermined after a century of liberal development. In this sense, Gamio's anthropological critique of classic liberal institutions was in the ideological vanguard of a movement that brought about forms of populism and corporate citizenship that had an immense impact on the course of politics in the twentieth century.

D. RACE AND *MESTIZAJE*

The mass politics that accompanied the rise of the revolutionary state was charged with a "mestizophilia" that has been cited by many scholars as a signature element of Latin American nationalism at the turn of the nineteenth century (Miller 2004). As was the case with culture, Gamio's discussions of race involve a tension between relativistic approaches borrowed from Boas and the political exigencies of a project that demanded national unity and homogeneity. In *Forjando Patria,* Gamio applied concepts from physical and cultural anthropology to proclaim the general biological and intellectual equality of the Indian population—but also to assert a need to promote race mixing. His emphasis on what sometimes looks like racial engineering has led some scholars to look for intellectual influences linking Gamio to representatives of the eugenics movement (see Castañeda 2003; Walsh 2004). Still, the particular uses of the idea of race in *Forjando Patria* and Gamio's other early writings tell a somewhat more complicated story. Although Gamio's commitments to biological anthropology varied over the course of his career, instances of race science in *Forjando Patria* involve a very fuzzy concept of heredity and somatology that hint at the ambivalent relationship between mestizophilic intellectuals and mainstream eugenics in the early twentieth century.

Gamio was clearly aware of eugenics research and seems to have perceived parallels between this and his own promotion of mestizaje. As Alexandra Stern has noted, he was elected vice-president of the Second International Eugenics Congress in 1920 (in Lomnitz 2001: 312) and was one of several Mexicans to receive subscriptions to U.S. eugenics journals. It is likely, however, that Gamio would have found much of the content of these texts and conferences to be difficult to reconcile with his own anthropological project. A heterogeneous movement, North American eugenics included both scholars that espoused racial relativism and others that fundamentally disapproved of race mixing or roundly dismissed the "racial potential" of Mexicans (see Lomnitz 2001: 139–140). Thus, although Gamio is known to have written assertions that "eugenics has as its objective the pursuing of racial improvement of human groups . . . [and] the heterogeneity of the Mexican population [makes imperative] the application of this science to Mexico" (in Tenorio Trillo 1999: 1176), it is unclear how his own understanding of this concept related to contemporaneous research being conducted in the United States. For example, nothing could be further from Gamio's promotion of race mixing than the work of prominent eugenicists Charles Davenport and Morris Steggerda, who published a widely read and cited work on Jamaica that ascribed a panoply of disharmonious physical and mental traits to Jamaican mulattoes (1929; see Comas 1961).

In contrast to the term "culture," which Gamio made obvious efforts to define, the term "race" appears in *Forjando Patria* as a common-sense and often ambiguous concept. This is one case in which it seems that Gamio's writing was more consistent with the folk definitions and genre expectations of his middlebrow readers. Race is probably the most common category used to contrast indigenous and European peoples by Latin American essayists and historians since the first half of the nineteenth century, a tradition that formed a significant part of the intellectual substrate of *Forjando Patria*. In contrast to the genetic definition used in twentieth-century eugenics, this essayistic tradition constituted different races as a concatenation of language, blood, and spirit (Stocking 1968: 65; Sierra O'Rielly 2002 [1861]; Chuchiak 1997). This romantic notion of race was at the heart of more humanistic discussions of *mestizaje* such as José Vasconcelos's *La Raza Cósmica* (1926) and is almost certainly how many nonspecialist readers in Mexico would have initially understood mentions of race in *Forjando Patria*. Gamio seems to have consciously used this more romantic register in some of the essays, such as in his references to a "poor and pained race" in Chapter 4 ("The Redemption of the Indigenous Class"). Other moments in the text show a blurring of boundaries between language, culture, and biology that is consistent with this romantic race concept, such as the discussion of the physical features and dialectical particularities of white Yucatecans in Chapter 23 ("Language and Our Country").

Other uses of the word "race" in *Forjando Patria* seem more consistent with the racial relativism of Boas and his students. This is evident when Gamio makes the assertion that "the Indian has intellectual qualities comparable to those of any race" (p. 36) or makes a nurture-over-nature argument regarding different cultural aptitudes:

> [A]ll human groups possess equal intellectual aptitudes in equal conditions
> of education and environment. To impose a certain culture or civilization
> on an individual or group, one must give them the necessary education and
> place them in the appropriate environment. (p. 39)

It is not clear, however, if Gamio's notion of race as biological makeup necessarily had the same implications of genetic inheritance that were at the core eugenics and early twentieth-century forms of physical anthropology. In some cases, Gamio refers to phenomena that seem to be cultural or environmental as defining the biological features of the "Indian race." For example, he notes that the patterns of muscular development that can physically distinguish persons of "Indian race" from those of "white race" were the result of diet and environmental factors (p. 132). This seems to imply that the somatic features that define the two "races" were derived from non-hereditary factors. This fuzzy concept of race often contributes to what seem like circular arguments. For example, an article that Gamio published in 1929 in the Santa Fe magazine *Palacio* opens with the assertion that race mixing was a means of avoiding a "race war" by eliminating the perceived bases for racism (see Gamio 1929). This implies that biological admixture was simply a means of checking prejudices that had a fundamentally cultural or social origin.

In the end, we can read the discussion of explicitly racial admixture in *Forjando Patria* as a largely metaphorical and analytically minor aspect of an intellectual manifesto that placed more emphasis on researching the cultural and linguistic dimensions of *mestizaje*. To some extent, we can see Gamio's discussions of race as answering to distinct genre expectations among his readers. Many who were familiar with social and biological sciences associated the term "anthropology" with nineteenth-century anthropometry and the study of physical characteristics. And for the vast majority of Gamio's Mexican readers, any discussion of *mestizaje* was likely to evoke a much longer national tradition of writing about mixtures of race or blood. It is also easy to imagine that this fuzzy definition of race reflects the anxieties of a Mexican scholar trying to engage a body of literature that enjoyed considerable international prestige but whose authors had often claimed to provide incontrovertible scientific proof of the constitutional inferiority of his countrymen.

E. THE FATE OF NATIONALIST ANTHROPOLOGY

The role of anthropology as an applied social science, an emphasis on the assimilation of indigenous people into a homogeneous national culture, and the use of archaeology as a collective representation of national identity all were signature features of the theory and practice of Mexican anthropology through the 1960s. All of these topics also became points of contention within a series of crises in Mexican anthropology and nationalism that marked the last third of the twentieth century. As an integral part of the state that emerged from the revolution, the vision of a nationalist anthropology proposed by Gamio was strongly implicated in the cultural legitimization of seventy years of single-party authoritarianism that developed in the decades that followed. Whereas the crisis that developed in Anglo-American anthropology in the 1980s is broadly attributed to doubts about the nature of representation, a somewhat earlier period of irony and introspection for Mexican anthropologists is intimately tied to the slow and painful decline of single-party rule.

Roger Bartra, an anthropologist who has written a series of particularly poignant analyses of the emergence and decay of the revolutionary cultural project, cites the violent repression of student protests in 1968 as a blow to the legitimacy of the Mexican state that ushered in a new period of popular discontent (Bartra 2002a: esp. 78–132; 2002b). The generation of radicalized students who saw many of their members shot down in the Tlatelolco massacre also produced a series of biting critiques of Mexico's "official" anthropology and cultural project. Texts like the volume *Eso que llaman la antropología mexicana* ("That which they call Mexican Anthropology" [Warman 1970]) took aim at the complicity of applied social science with the modernizing schemes of the authoritarian state and the ultimate failure of policies meant to improve the lives of Mexico's indigenous people. Gamio and his immediate successors were seen not as revolutionaries but as the inheritors of an ethnocentric modernizing ethos that denied political and cultural self-determination to indigenous groups. Likewise, archaeologists took aim at the dogmatism, theoretical stagnation, and general "officialism" of the "monumental restoration school" (Matos Moctezuma 1979; Rodríguez Garcia 1997).

Many of the critics who had participated in the protests and polemics of 1968 were initially expelled or otherwise marginalized within state-controlled academic institutions. But, in a gesture that would be repeated again and again when the legitimacy of the Mexican state came into crisis, some of these scholars were eventually incorporated into government posts, ranging from the head of the INAH to the secretariat of agriculture. Against the backdrop of financial collapse and neoliberal reforms in the 1980s and 1990s, their impact as public intellectuals was mixed (see Lomnitz 2001). Still, the broad critique of Mexican anthropology contributed to an academic culture in which moving forward implied a criticism of the institutional culture that emerged within the revolutionary state. By the 1980s, widely read books such as Guillermo Bonfil Batalla's *México Profundo* (1996) pushed the critique of the assimilationist policies and revolutionary nationalism of the early twentieth century into the mainstream.

By the time that seven decades of single-party rule ended with the 2000 presidential election, other political and cultural crises had further disrupted the vision of anthropology and national culture articulated by Gamio in 1916. The 1994 rebellion of the Ejército Zapatista de Liberacíon Nacional (EZLN, Zapatista Army of National Liberation) in the impoverished state of Chiapas underscored the deep fractures that still existed in national society and represented a new kind of movement that mobilized indigenous identity in opposition to the neoliberal development and authoritarian policies of the Mexican state. "Good government," a term used extensively by Gamio to refer to state policies that were informed by an anthropological knowledge of the populace, now tends to evoke the rhetoric of neo-Zapatismo and the autonomous zones founded and protected by the movement's leadership. Once again, the Mexican state ultimately faced this political crisis by entering into a dialogue and attempting to incorporate the Zapatista agenda into an "official" multiculturalism. Although the results of this dialogue ultimately proved unsatisfactory to the Zapatistas themselves, reforms that were instituted in the national constitution reversed decades of assimilationist policy and declared that Mexican nationhood was based on a multiethnic and multicultural society.

CONCLUSIONS

What does a text like *Forjando Patria*, which embodies a particular moment of nationalism and anthropology for a very specific geographical context, offer to a more general understanding of the history of anthropology? It is almost too obvious to state that the study of anthropological traditions from the global south often lends a new perspective to the universalist assumptions of First World social sciences. A more specific reflection can be derived from the comparison of Mexican and U.S. anthropologists, members of a community of scholars that shared a common set of theoretical assumptions and research projects in the 1910s but that trained subsequent generations of students who experienced radically different social roles and expectations (see Tenorio Trillo 1999; Lomnitz 2001). The divergent trajectories of these two traditions come into sharp relief when we contrast the fin-de-siècle crises that faced each. Gamio's nationalist vision of anthropology fell victim to the slow loss of political legitimacy that ultimately brought an end to single-party authoritarianism. In contrast, the crisis of the "classical norms" (Rosaldo 1989) of North American anthropology hinged on reflections about the discipline's complicity with colonial and neo-colonial institutions that seemed to be at a more comfortable distance from the ivory tower of research universities.

Gamio's references to a broad range of topics and to the specific political concerns of his time are reminders that differences in national traditions are not simply a divergence in ideas but also a difference in the social context of anthropological practice (see Patterson 2001). Gamio's attempt to reconcile the core principles of a university-based tradition from the United States with a different model of public intellectuality and a socially engaged nationalist project set the tone for an institutional logic that defined the experience of future generations of Mexican anthropologists. The compromises that he made between relativism and assimilation are not simply the result of provincial pragmatism or postcolonial anxieties but part of a far more concrete concatenation of bureaucratic practices, political paternalism, scientific expertise, and technical stewardship.

In this sense, *Forjando Patria* is not simply a document of what anthropology became in early twentieth-century Mexico but of what anthropology *can become* when it develops in an institutional context that gives its practitioners a more direct engagement in the formulation of public education and other aspects of cultural policy within a populist state. In contrast, the struggle of many anthropologists in the United States to find new forms of engagement with the public reflects the heritage of a discipline whose traditional study of "primitives" in exotic parts of the world constituted an object of analysis that was removed from the everyday realities of university life. The legacy of Manuel Gamio exists somewhere between these two traditions, in the experimentation of archaeological methods that contributed to avowedly disinterested research conducted around the world and in the articulation of a nationalist social science tailor-made for revolutionary Mexico. His own life, as student, ideologue and exile, further demonstrates the interplay between different national spaces and the roles ascribed to social scientists as ivory tower scholars or public intellectuals. This makes a better understanding of his life and works an important step in developing a comparative perspective on the diverse histories of anthropology in North and South.

NOTES ON THE TRANSLATION

Translating a text like *Forjando Patria* offers a series of unique challenges. Foremost among these is the question of narrative register in which the text was written. The essays that make up this book were originally written for a middlebrow audience, in a style more akin to essayism and creative nonfiction than what most readers today would consider to be an anthropological article. Translating these essays involved a careful negotiation between providing a readable and informative text and giving the reader the experience that this is, in fact, a period-specific narrative. For the sake of readability, I have divided many long and complicated sentences into shorter ones, deleted some repetitive rhetorical flourishes, and in some cases changed the order of sentences within paragraphs. The result is a text that will be more comprehensible to contemporary readers but that still conveys a very different reading experience from much contemporary anthropological writing. In some cases, I have translated key terms and arguments in terms that were common in the writing of Gamio's Anglophone contemporaries but that might seem quaint to contemporary readers. I have left some words, like the crucial word *patria* ("fatherland"), untranslated. All notes to the text are in the original except those explicitly marked "Trans."

Manuel Gamio's *Forjando Patria* (1916)

I

Forjando Patria

In the great forge of America, on the anvil of the Andes, the bronze and iron of virile races have been alloyed for centuries and centuries.

When the task of mixing and blending peoples came to the brown arms of Atahualpa and Moctezuma, a miraculous tie was consummated. The same blood swelled the veins of the Americans, and their intellectuality flowed through the same paths. There were small *patrias*: the Aztec, the Maya-Kiché, the Inca . . . that would later perhaps have grouped together and melded into great indigenous *patrias*, as the *patrias* of China and Japan were in the same age. But it could not be thus. When other men, another blood, other ideas arrived with Columbus, the crucible that unified the race was tragically overturned and the mold in which the Nationality was created and the *Patria* crystallized fell to pieces.

During the colonial centuries, the first forges of noble nationalist impulses also burned, only the Pizarros and Ávilas just intended to build incomplete *patrias*, since they valued only the steel of the Latin race, leaving the crude indigenous bronze on the slag heap.

Later on, imitating the most brilliant of previous centuries, Olympic men took up the epic and sonorous hammer, clothed themselves with the glorious smith's apron. They were Bolívar, Morelos, Hidalgo, San Martín, Sucre[1] . . .

---

[1] Simon Bolívar (1783–1830), Miguel Hidalgo y Costilla (1753–1811), José María Morelos (1756–1815), José Francisco de San Martín (1778–1850), Antonio José de Sucre (1799–1830).—Trans.

they went to scale the mountain, to strike the divine anvil, to forge with blood and gunpowder, with muscles and ideas, with hope and disenchantment, a peregrine statue made of the metals that are all of the races of America. For various decades, a thunderous hammering that made the high mountain ranges tremble could be heard, stirring virgin fronds of new life and making the twilight red, as if blood splattered even the heavens. In Panama, where oceans and continents kiss, the marvelous image of the great American *Patria* was glimpsed as if in an epic poem. Single and great, serene and majestic like the Andean mountain chain.

But the time had not yet come. The miracle unmade itself. That sublime vision of *patria* was lost like sea-foam or the fog of the mountaintops. Those men who today are longed for, like Homeric demigods, passed on to a better life.

A new idea came later, during the independent life of those countries. No longer would there be a single gigantic *patria* that would bring all of the men of the continent together as one. Rather, looking to past tradition, powerful *patrias* would be formed that corresponded to colonial political divisions. Unfortunately, the nature of this task was not well understood by the forgers. There was an attempt to sculpt the statue of those *patrias* with Latin racial elements, leaving the indigenous race in a dangerous oblivion. If the indigenous race was remembered at all, in the name of mercy, a humble bronze pedestal was made with it. Ultimately, what must happen did. The statue, inconsistent and fragile, fell many times, while the pedestal grew. And that struggle, which has sustained itself in making a *patria* and nationality for more than a century, is at the root of our civil contentions.

It is now the task of the revolutionaries of Mexico to take up the hammer and tie on the apron of the forger to make a new *patria* of intermixed iron and bronze surge from the miraculous anvil. There is the iron. . . . There is the bronze. . . . Stir, brothers!

2

Patrias and Nationalities of Latin America

With few exceptions, one does not find the characteristics that are inherent in a defined and integrated nationality in most Latin American countries. In these countries, there is neither a generalized idea nor a unanimous feeling of what a *Patria* is. Instead, there are small *patrias* and local nationalisms.

This state of affairs is evident at the occasional congresses that bring together the representatives of these countries. The Second Pan-American Scientific Conference and the XIX Congress of Americanists, held in Washington, D.C., last December and January, provided an interesting and ample field in which to observe this point. As a whole, the delegations attending both congresses represented the race, language, and culture of no more than 25 percent of the populations of their respective countries. They represented the Spanish and Portuguese languages and the race and civilization of European origin. The remaining 75 percent of those populations, composed of men of indigenous race, indigenous language, and indigenous civilization, was not represented. A few researchers at the conference mentioned this indigenous population, but only in ethnological terms, as the object of scholarly speculation. In a sense, the existence of these 75 million Americans goes unnoticed by all of the so-called civilized world. The languages that they speak are unknown; we are ignorant of their physical nature and of their ethical and religious ideas. Their habits and customs are unknown to us.

Can countries in which the two main components of the population are so different from each other in all respects, and are completely ignorant of each other, be considered *patrias*? To further develop these ideas and the conclusions that can be derived from them, we will summarize the characteristics of nationality and the conditions inherent in the concept of *patria*.

A. *PATRIAS* AND NATIONALITIES

If one observes countries that possess a defined and integrated nationality (Germany, France, Japan, and so forth), one finds the following conditions. First, there is the ethnic unity of the majority of the population. That is, the population is composed of individuals who belong to the same race or to ethnic types that are very closely related to each other. Second, the majority of each of these populations has and uses a common language, unprejudiced by the presence of secondary languages or dialects. Third, diverse elements, classes, or social groups in these countries manifest aspects of the same culture, however much these manifestations differ in their form or intensity depending on the economic conditions or the physical and intellectual development of said groups. In other words, the majority of the population has similar ideas, albeit with variations in form. They share similar sentiments and express similar aesthetic, moral, religious, and political ideals. Housing, eating habits, dress, and all customs in general are the same, with differences simply being an indicator of the better or worse economic conditions of different social classes. Finally, memory of the past—with all of its glories and tears—is treasured in the hearts of all like a holy relic. National traditions, that ancient pedestal on which the *Patria* rests, live vibrantly and vigorously in the minds of men, women, and children. They are shared by the wise and the ignorant, by the sons of the rabble and among the most refined, by the highest cultivators of art and the poor village storyteller. That kind of national tradition performs the miracle of transmuting itself into a thousand different faces, while always conserving its unity and typical character.

The Germans, the French, the Japanese, those who possess a true nationality, are children of one great family. When they travel through their respective countries, they find true brethren among men, women, and children. They rise to the solemn cry of the same blood, of the same flesh. That cry is the voice of life, the mysterious force that groups together matter and opposes its disintegration. In the souls of all of these people, one finds the same images that are in one's own soul. From their lips the words of a single language spill forth, aged like fine wine. When one lives in this way, one has a *Patria*.

We will now see if the countries that stretch from the Rio Bravo to the Straits of Magellan are *patrias* in the same way. Because the characteristics and general conditions of almost all of the Latin American countries are similar, we will focus on Mexico as a country that is representative of the others.

B. MEXICO AS A COUNTRY REPRESENTATIVE OF LATIN AMERICA

Before listing and considering the little *patrias* that exist within Mexico, we shall analyze their basic features.

1. *Race, Language, and Civilization.* Can 8 or 10 million individuals of indigenous race, language, and culture hold the same ideals and aspirations, have the same goals, revere the same *patria*, and treasure the same nationalistic sentiments as 4 or 6 million persons of European origin who inhabit the same territory but speak a different language, belong to a different race, and think in accordance with the teachings of a different culture or civilization? We think not. We find a certain similarity between this situation and that of the former South African republics. These were countries in which political franchise was always limited to the population of European origins and in which the indigenous peoples were relegated to servitude and passivity. There and in the other European colonies in Africa, European man and European civilization suffocate and will ultimately extinguish indigenous life in all of its manifestations.

The separation and divergence of our great social groups (indigenous and European) already existed during the Conquest and the Colonial age, but they are more profound in contemporary times. We can admit, casting aside hypocritical reservations, that our national independence was attained by the group of European origins. This group sought material and intellectual liberties and progress for itself, leaving the indigenous group to its own destiny. This happened in spite of the fact that the indigenous group is more numerous and probably possesses greater energies and physical endurance as a result of its particular forms of culture.

At first glance, the situation that we have described seems frightening. Those ill with "sociological myopia" might glimpse the beginnings of a fearful caste war in which the advantage would probably not go to the population of European origin. Such fears would be unfounded. Today, the indigenous population is divided into more or less numerous groups that constitute small *patrias*, much as they did at the time of the Conquest. These small *patrias* are bound together by race, language, and culture. Their mutual rivalries and indifference toward one another facilitated the Conquest during the sixteenth century and led to their cultural stagnation during the Colonial period and the present day.

The problem is not, then, to prevent an imaginary mass aggression by our indigenous groups, but to mobilize their disparate energies toward a common goal. Therefore, the task at hand is to bring these individuals closer to that social group whom they have always considered to be an enemy, to incorporate them into it, to blend them with it. Our end should be to make the national race homogeneous, unify the language, and make the different cultures that exist in our country converge into one.

It might be deduced from what we have argued above that we believe that the inhabitants of Mexico who possess race, language, and culture of European origin constitute a *patria* or nationality. However, this hypothesis is also untenable. Besides the anthropological factors discussed before, geography plays an important role in creating small *patrias*. The primary reason why Mexico lost the territory that is currently in the hands of the United States is that there is a vast geographic distance between said territory and the rest of the country. Along with this distance came divergence and even antagonism between the nationalist ideals of persons from different regions.

Twenty years ago in the state of Chiapas—before the construction of the Pan-American Railway—the population of white race tended to have a stronger sense of national affiliation with Central America than with Mexico. Habits, customs, commercial relations, intellectual culture—almost everything—bore the stamp of those other countries, especially of Guatemala. Could the inhabitants of Baja California, particularly the northern part, have the same sense of patriotism as those of us who live in the rest of the country? Do they not see themselves forced to cross into foreign territory more often than they set foot in the continental part of their own *patria*? What stamp do commerce, intellectuality, dress, and all the activities of life have in this northern state? It must be confessed that the resident of Mexico City would find these regions to be absolutely exotic, Yankee-ized.

2. *The Economic Aspect.* For a family to live in harmonious unity, all of its members must enjoy economic resources that can provide them with physical and intellectual well-being. For a group of families to form a harmonic whole, to constitute a nationality, it is essential that all enjoy the well-being that can only be obtained through an equitable economic situation. As always happens in Mexico, some few families live amidst abundance and most others suffer the torment of hunger, nakedness, and intellectual abandon. In this situation, an artificial union of different groups would not result in a harmonic whole. A nationality cannot surge in a country where the idea of personal preservation has prevailed above any sense of having a patria.

3. *The Political System.* It is said that independent Mexico is ruled by a representative democracy. This is not so in reality, because the indigenous classes have been forced to live under the rule of laws that are not derived from their necessities, but from those of the population of European origin, whose necessities are very different.

C. THE SMALL *PATRIAS* OF MEXICO

If a person from the capital who possesses language, race, and culture of European origin goes to Yucatán, Quintana Roo, Chiapas, or to the lands of the Yaqui and the Huichol, he finds himself in an environment that is stranger to him than that of some European countries. Language, physical appearance, habits, customs, ideals, aspirations, hopes, and entertainments are all different. These small *patrias* can be divided into two groups: those whose population is exclusively indigenous and others whose populations show the harmonic fusion of the indigenous race and the race of European origin.

1. Patrias *of Indigenous Population.* One can mention those already cited: the Maya, Yaqui, and Huichol. These are groups that possess a nationality that is clearly marked by their respective languages and by their cultural and physical natures. Their natures are and have always been unknown to groups of European origin, with the exception of a very small number of Mexican and foreign anthropologists. This ignorance is an unpardonable crime against Mexican nationhood. Without knowing the characteristics and needs of those groups, it is impossible to seek their incorporation into a national culture.

2. *Yucatán, a Type of* Patria *of Mixed Population.* A few months ago, after having toured that state, I stayed awhile in Mérida. On one occasion, when I was having lunch at a restaurant in the city center, it occurred to me to order a bottle of beer.

I was asked, "Domestic or foreign?"

"Foreign," I answered, imagining that I would be served a German or American beer. A few instants later, the waiter returned, bringing on a bright tray a bottle of XX of Orizaba.

"I had said foreign!" I exclaimed, a bit annoyed.

The dark-skinned waiter looked at me with good-natured surprise and replied: "It is the only foreign beer we have. If you want a domestic one, I will bring you a Yucatecan beer."

Nationalist in the extreme and at times patriotic to the point of aggression, I could not help but inform my interlocutor of two or three politico-geographic facts about Yucatán and Mexico, and four or five about the lack of sense that he seemed to suffer from. To the shame of my metropolitan pride, that poor waiter gave me so many and such justified reasons that in the end I understood—for all that I did not approve of it—why the beer of Orizaba was considered foreign in Yucatán.

I will now demonstrate why Yucatán is one of our small *patrias* and why it possesses its own nationalist sensibility. In the Yucatecan territory, the conquered indigenous race and the invading Spanish race have mixed more harmoniously and deeply than in any other region of the republic. Although there are some people of pure Indian or European blood, enough of a social majority is of mixed race to make this the dominant group. The distinctiveness is so evident that even when a Yucatecan does not state the place of his provenience, this can be deduced by simply hearing his voice. The pronounced brachycephaly of the cranium, like the peculiar phoneticism of his pronunciation, loudly proclaims his Yucatecan origins. This racial homogeneity, this unification of physical type, this advanced and happy fusion of the races, constitutes the primary and solid base of Yucatecan nationalism.

Let us now examine language, which is the next most important factor of nationalist identity in Yucatán. There, the immense majority of the rural population speaks the Maya language, and the majority of the urban population speaks Spanish. This means that all of the inhabitants of the state can communicate in one language or the other. This does not happen in any other region of the republic.

As far as customs, one notes convergences that, despite seeming trivial, are a basis for nationalism. All Yucatecans, from the wealthiest henequen planter to the humble cutter of the same fiber, wear the same white outfit with the same straw hat. These articles only vary in quality. I would not say that this is simply a function of the tropical climate, as one does not find this uniformity in dress in parts of the republic that are even hotter. The same can be said for the hammock, which is used by all in the peninsula. There is also a pronounced regionalism in decoration and dance. Cleanliness, the daily bath, is an inherent characteristic of all the population, the lack of water notwithstanding. Finally, it might surprise many in the capital to know that a Yucatecan national anthem has been composed and is often played in that region.

All of the diverse social classes of Yucatán share an understandable antiforeign sentiment, which is permissible insofar as it does not become hostility or aggression. Yucatán is one of the states in which the fewest foreigners reside. Because of this, capital, industry, agriculture, means of communication, and so forth are completely national. The isolation of Yucatán contributes much to the development of its nationalism. It is bordered by the waters of the Gulf of Mexico for much of its extension and by unexplored regions of Quintana Roo to the south. It is only linked with the republic and with foreign countries through two or three of its ports and the railway that leads to Campeche.

Let us now examine the relations that exist between Yucatán and the rest of the republic. The only people who went from Mexico to Yucatán before the revolution were the promoters of pornographic theater, soldiers, and forced laborers. There were also those people with the title of federal employees who went to round out their own bellies by striking the locals where it hurts most: in the pocket. When has Yucatan ever seen the flower of Mexican capitalists, professionals, and artists? Never! The rich state was treated like the hen that lays golden eggs. Its citizens were never given sympathy, material or intellectual help, or the love of brothers and compatriots. Is it now clear why Yucatecans constitute a small *patria* and why they have always held on to a legitimate sense of nationalism?

3

The Department of Anthropology

It is a given that anthropology, in its true and amplest conception, should be the basic form of knowledge for good government. Through anthropology, one gains awareness of the population that is the source of both rulers and those who are ruled over. Through anthropology, one can characterize the abstract and physical nature of men and peoples and deduce the appropriate methods to facilitate their normal evolutionary development.

Unfortunately, the necessities of the different peoples that inhabit our country have been unknown to the government and public. The same problem is evident in almost all of the Latin American countries. Because of this, the evolution of these countries has been abnormal. The minority formed by people whose race and civilization are derived from Europe has furthered its own development, abandoning the majority made up of people of indigenous race and culture. In some cases, that abandonment was intentional. But even in those rare cases where the population of European race and civilization attempted to bring about the economic and cultural betterment of the indigenous majority, they did so without knowing its nature, its way of being, its aspirations and needs. Their failures have taught us that some means of bettering the conditions of the indigenous population are inappropriate and ill-informed. Our ignorance results from the fact that the indigenous population has not been studied sensibly. The national population has but few contacts with them, through commercial interactions or by engaging the indigenous population in different forms of servitude. The indigenous soul, culture, and ideals are therefore unknown to us.

The only way of comprehending the physical type, civilization, and language of the diverse indigenous families that populate our national soil is through the investigation of their pre-colonial and colonial antecedents with an anthropological sensibility. But having established the capital importance of anthropology for Latin American countries, we must first determine how those countries are to be investigated anthropologically. When we compare anthropological studies that have been conducted in our countries with the advanced state that this science has attained in Europe and the United States, it becomes evident that our own results have been deficient. Our investigators have lacked mutual understanding and intellectual exchange. Our investigations have lacked rigorous methodology and harmonic synthesis.

Mexico, the country of America that offers the most copious anthropological material, and where the first empirical investigations were conducted, is a concrete example of this problem. In Mexico, investigations in ethnography, archaeology, linguistics, folklore, and other anthropological subjects began in the sixteenth century, when Sahagún, Durán, Alva Ixtlilxóchitl, Cortés, Bernal Díaz, and other colonial chroniclers collected very interesting data of anthropological character. If we were to consider these data through contemporary scientific criteria, they appear isolated and unconnected. They are purely descriptive and of little scientific significance. But, of course, those colonial writers cannot be held at fault, since their goal was to write history, not to conduct anthropological investigations. Unfortunately, the shortcomings of these early investigations persisted in later periods.

When the nineteenth century arrived, anthropology acquired a scientific character. Hardworking investigators who are still among us began to conduct research during that period. The task that these men accomplished was twofold. First, they conducted original work consisting of new empirical investigations. Second, they conducted a work of reconsideration, which consisted of bringing modern lights to the data of colonial investigators. But even when the studies engendered by these two tasks were conducted with the best scientific discipline, they continued to lack unified methods and harmonic synthesis as a body of research. Like the ethnological, archaeological, historical, and folkloric investigations conducted during the Colonial period, they remain disconnected, ineloquent, and of a purely descriptive character.

At present, we can say that a few of our indigenous families have been studied anthropologically and that some attention has also been conceded to the social elements of European origin. But these investigations have in no way remedied our lack of general and official knowledge about the population. We will try to explain the causes of this failure.

Let us suppose that one intends to gain anthropological knowledge of the great Otomí family that has lived in the high mesas since the remote past. Following the procedures that have been used until now, the investigator would first go to a little village made up of individuals of Otomí speech. He would then establish the filiation of these individuals in accordance with a correct ethnological methodology. Having done this, he would see to it that the manuscript generated by his investigation appeared in a specialized publication. With this, he would be satisfied with his work and consider it to be finished. He would then go on to study the Zapotec individuals of this town or the Tepehuanes of that other one.

What transcendence can such a study have beyond its individual value as an isolated document? What use is such an investigation when it is not supported by ethnological studies of the thousands of Otomí that live in other villages or by complementary physiographic, biological, archaeological, historical, and statistical/demographic studies? Is it not also indispensable to analyze the intercultural influences and crossings of blood produced by four centuries of Spanish presence among the Otomís?

When the way of being of the great Otomí family is known scientifically and when the causes that have brought about that way of being are determined, we come closer to the ultimate practical goals of anthropological study. It is necessary to determine the current needs of that great family, to deduce and develop immediate means to remedy those needs, and to establish a scientific means of monitoring that family's development in order to promote its future physical and intellectual well-being.

To illustrate this way of practicing anthropology, we will refer to the problem of labor among the Otomís. Investigations could demonstrate whether the productive capacity of the Otomí is normal or abnormal and if the abnormality is motivated by physical incompetence or if it results from conscious will. In either case, the causes of the phenomenon will be studied, with a particular focus on the individuals' nutrition, the biological environment in which they develop, and the work that they do. Afterward, it would be possible to remedy the causes of abnormal production in political and economic terms.

When this process is applied to the incorporation of our indigenous families into national life, the forces that have kept the country in a latent and passive state will be transformed into dynamic productive energies. This will fortify the feeling of nationalism that is currently dissipated by divergences in the ethnic types, languages, cultural concepts, and tendencies of the different social groups that make up our population. To reach such ends, the Mexican government plans to create a Department of Anthropology or Central Anthropological Institute. This institute will study the national population according to rigorous anthropological criteria and from the following points of view:

1st Quantitatively: Statistics.

2nd Qualitatively: Physical type, language, and civilization or culture.

3rd Chronologically: Pre-colonial period, Colonial, and contemporary.

4th Environmental conditions: Regional physiobiology.

We ask this cultured congress to recommend the creation of institutions analogous to the one just described in the numerous American countries in which the nature and necessities of the population make them necessary. In this way, the nationalities of America would be enlarged, fortified, and stabilized, and Panamericanism will be truly effective.

4

. . . .

The Redemption of the Indigenous Class

Nine years ago, the author of this book attempted to publish articles in several Mexico City newspapers to criticize the "personal contributions" or "*derechos de capitación*" that survived in many states of the republic as a bitter relic of long-gone encomiendas. All of the newspapers refused to comment on the issue. The author was nevertheless able to publish the following lines in the magazine *Modern Mexico*, which was published in New York and circulated in Mexico.

"When I admire the great works of the Japanese people, their precocity, and inexhaustible energy, I must naturally contemplate the painful miseries that afflict our poor indigenous class.

"Viewing the ethnico-social characteristics of the Indian, one finds very important factors that could lead to his decisive and transcendent regeneration.

"One is surprised by the Indians' vitality as much as by their vigorous physical nature. Their physiology is intriguing, since we find very few countries in which the human body is so productive in spite of a lack of nutrition. Also, the Indian has intellectual qualities comparable to those of any race.

"At the same time, the Indian is timid and lacks energy and aspirations. He lives in constant fear of the scorn and demands of the 'people of reason,' of the white man. He still bows his head to his torturer, to him who raised the hobnailed boot of the conquering Castilian.

"Poor and pained race! In your breast hides the strength of the tough Tarahumara who fells cedar in the mountain, the exquisite art of the divine

36

Teotihuacano, the sagacity of the Tlaxcallan family, the indomitable bravery of the bloody Mexica. Why do you not hold your head up high, proud to show the world your Indian heritage?

"Poor and pained race! You were oppressed for centuries by a doubly tyrannical yoke. First, there was the pagan fanaticism with which you deified your ancient king-priests. Second, the brutal egoism of the conquerors that always drowned the aspirations of the inferior class. You will not awaken spontaneously, however healthy and elevated you might be. It will be essential that friendly hearts work for your redemption.

"This great task should begin by erasing the eternal timidity that governs the Indian. We must make him understand, in a simple and objective fashion, that there is no longer any reason for him to fear us. He is our brother and will never again be a pariah. Arduous efforts will be needed to inculcate this elementary civic thought into his brain. It will also be necessary to abolish, among other things, that black vestige of the past, that relic of the encomiendas: the head tax.

"Once the Indian finds himself exempt from this 'contribution for living' and feels himself to be a man, once he has confidence, he will begin to attend school. A rudimentary initiative will suffice to make him look to broader horizons. We should all help in our respective spheres to see how to bring these beautiful ideals into fruition. Next, we will make the reader familiar with an initiative that was proposed in the capital of one of our border states for the benefit of this devalued race."

5

Prejudices against the Indigenous Race and Its History

In *The Mind of Primitive Man*, an interesting work in which Dr. Franz Boas compiles his lectures from Harvard and Mexico, the chapter on racial prejudices is especially worthy of attention. The illustrious professor condemns prejudices regarding the aptitudes of different human groups and proves that the innate inferiority that is ascribed to some groups does not exist. Deficiencies in aptitude are produced by historical, biological, and geographic causes; that is, by education and environment. When these causes are changed, perceived inferiorities disappear. It is indispensable that such logical ideas should be popularized among us, as we are a nation composed of ethnically heterogeneous social groups, each of which has developed along divergent paths. Our progress as a nation has not been synchronous.

The great problem of studying Mexico's indigenous families and their future has always been addressed with naïve and superficial prejudices. There are those who see the indigenous social group as a barrier to the progress of the whole, as an element that is resistant to all culture and destined to perish like a sterile field in which no seed flourishes. They believe that this justifies the unfortunate state in which the Indian has lived for four centuries. At the other extreme, those who practice and preach the work of Indianism exalt the capacities of the Indian beyond all limits, considering him superior to Europeans in intellectual and physical aptitudes. They say that if the Indian had not been trapped and oppressed by foreign races, he would now supersede the European in culture. They use Juarez, Altamirano,[1] and other isolated cases of illustrious Indians to support their opinions.

[1]   Benito Juarez (1806–1872), Ignacio Manuel Altamirano (1834–1893).—Trans.

Naturally, neither of these positions is correct. The Indian has the same aptitude for progress as the white; he is neither inferior nor superior. It happens that certain historical antecedents and very specific social, biological, and geographic conditions have made him unable to assimilate culture of European origin. If the overwhelming weight of these historical antecedents were to disappear, if the Indian were to forget three centuries of colonial oppressions and the hundred years of "independentist" oppressions, if he were no longer considered zoologically inferior to the white, if his nutrition, clothing, education, and living conditions were improved, the Indian would embrace contemporary culture in the same way as any individual of any other race.

In summary, it can be said that all human groups possess equal intellectual aptitudes in equal conditions of education and environment. To impose a certain culture or civilization on an individual or group, one must give them the necessary education and place them in the appropriate environment. Of course, this process is much easier in the case of an individual than with a group of individuals. With the simple transference of an individual to a distinct environment at a convenient age, negative historical antecedents can generally be overcome. This occurs with the indigenous children from Spanish America that are sent to Europe to acquire the modalities of European intellectual culture. They would return to Mexico as perfect representatives of European culture, if human arrogance did not fixate on their pigmentation. Social groups, on the other hand, present a great resistance toward changes in civilization, even when they are transferred en masse to a different environment. This can be seen in the nomadic tribes of Arabia, Turkey, Bohemia, and other places, which have migrated all over the world without changing their physical type, customs, and language.

There are two primary reasons why European civilization has not been able to impose itself onto our indigenous population. First, there is the natural resistance that the indigenous population presents to any change in its culture. Second, the imposition of European civilization has failed because we do not know the reasons for the Indians' resistance. We do not know how the Indian thinks, and we ignore his true aspirations. We prejudge him with our own sensibilities, when we should familiarize ourselves with his sensibilities in order to comprehend him and make him comprehend us. We must forge for ourselves—even if temporarily—an Indian soul. Then, we may work for the advancement of the indigenous class. This is not the task of the ruler or of the pedagogue, nor of the sociologist. It is first and foremost the task of the anthropologist, and particularly of the ethnologist. His apostolate requires not only illustration and abnegation but a perspective that is absolutely free from prejudices, especially racial prejudice.

Regarding the civilizations that inhabited Mexico before the Conquest, these prejudices against the Indian race are so great that they have contributed to an erroneous, fantastic, and inadmissible account of our own history. Even the facts presented in our textbooks are often erroneous, lacking in historical perspective, and presented without scientific methodology.

We can discuss the history of the pre-Hispanic civilizations of the Valley of Mexico as an example. National history texts name them a thousand different ways: Toltecs, Chichimecs, Colhua, Acolhua, Tepaneca, Nahuatlaca, and on and on. Historians debate the appropriateness of these different names, discard some, institutionalize others, and even invent some. When a student finishes the course or a reader turns the last page, he knows nothing about our pre-Columbian past. All that remains in his mind is a tangle of exotic-sounding indigenous words, the retention of which is as difficult as it is useless. In the end, the student or reader still ignores who these civilizations were and what they were really like. He ignores their religious concepts; works of art; religious, civil, and military institutions; industries; and so forth. Some history texts do refer to the religion, art, and customs of our pre-Hispanic inhabitants. But we would sincerely prefer that those texts not touch upon such issues, as their erroneous content disorients the reader.

The discussions of pre-Hispanic people in most history texts have been inconsistent, anachronistic, and obfuscated. Authors tend to mix together aspects of distinct cultures. Likewise, there is a tendency to confuse manifestations of culture that were still flowering at the arrival of Cortés with others that had disappeared thousands of years earlier. These two problems are evident in the list of names commonly given for the peoples of the Valley of Mexico. Historical texts give them more than ten different denominations but do nothing to describe them or distinguish them from other peoples. It is systematic archaeology (in this case, geologico-cultural stratigraphy) that has demonstrated objectively (through architecture, ceramics, sculpture, etc.) that three great civilizations existed in the Valley of Mexico. The profusion of denominations that history texts have so naïvely created must be forcefully melded into these three civilizations.

We should be concerned about deficiencies in the histories that we have written of colonial and independent Mexico. But the lack of concern that we have shown for the pre-Hispanic age is even more deplorable. This is a history that we have not even begun to write, in spite of the richness of the relevant material. This situation is inexcusable, given that pre-Hispanic history should constitute the base of colonial and contemporary history.

6

Sociology and Government

Sociologists observe and record social phenomena with a scientific methodology, but the laws that they attempt to deduce from these data are often anything but scientific. If they were, it would be possible to predict the occurrence of different social phenomena and to ensure the well-being of peoples, something that has been attempted since the beginning of time but that has never been achieved. These problems have emerged in all of the nations where true sociological investigations have been undertaken.

This situation is compounded in Mexico, where sociological laws have never been formulated. This is to be expected, given that this science has never been applied to our population through proper investigation and methods. But even if our rulers do not need scientifically tested social laws in order to govern, it is indispensable that they know the characteristics of the individuals and groups that they are to rule over, so that they might consistently attend to their necessities and seek their betterment.

When, for example, have we ever studied the nature of our different social classes through rigorous empirical observation? Usually, we classify them in broad strokes as high, middle, and lower class. In our popular speech, they are known as *pelados*, *decentes*, and *rotos*.[1] Ethnologists might refer to them as

---

[1] *Pelados* is a slang term that refers roughly to urban lumpenproletariat. *Decentes*, or "decent people," refers to respectable bourgeois. Although *roto* is a pejorative term for the poor in other parts of Latin America, Mexicans of Gamio's time used the term to refer to wealthy people with a pretentious or foppish manner.—Trans.

Indians, whites, and mestizos and engage in more profound discussions about the differences among the three. But even their observations are generally of little avail, as our rulers promote the well-being of the class to which they belong by birth—or of that into which they have been incorporated—and leave the others to stagnate. Dedicated exclusively to understanding his own social class, the ruler is prejudiced against the rest and is ignorant of their aspirations and needs. Thus, he neglects the study of sociological principles and applies inappropriate procedures to the government of the population.

Conflict has always existed between the so-called upper class, rich and powerful, and the lower, which is poor but has much greater material power. The middle class, the source of all of our intellectual activity, of the brains that are competent to lead, has lived in the midst of a constant struggle between the other two. All of this results from the fact that we, as different social groups that inhabit a single country, do not know each other. In the following pages we will propose some procedures that are necessary for attaining this knowledge.

7

Knowledge of the Population

It is not possible to determine the necessities of a people, or to seek their improvement, without knowing their statistics. Statistics is a systematic synthesis of the economic, ethnological, biological, and other characteristics of human groups. Knowing these characteristics leads to understanding the necessities of the population and how to address them. In Mexico, statistical studies have tended to focus on the quantitative evaluation of the population, almost never accounting for qualitative factors. This has been the cause for endless political failures.

The ruler should have the sociologist as his guide, and the work of the sociologist rests on the foundation of statistics. Statistics is itself founded on the harmonic integration of scientifically collected empirical data that are pertinent to economic, geographic, ethnological, and other phenomena. When one is forced to rely on isolated empirical data gathered in an unsystematic manner, statistics becomes like a commercial inventory that can only name and list individual objects. The sociologist is transformed into a juggler, because he uses meaningless and disconnected data to deduce social principles and laws that are useless in the real world. If the ruler rules without consulting such a sociologist, he rules badly. If he *does* consult him, his rule is even worse. It is less prejudicial to rule a people by serving their needs directly and superficially than by detailed plans based on disconcerting and ill-conceived conclusions.

Our leaders need to know much more than just the number of men, women, and children that live in the republic, or the languages that they speak, or how they are divided into different ethnic groups. Many other data need to be known about geography, geology, meteorology, fauna, and flora. These things must not be studied as isolated details, but in terms of how they relate to one another and to the habitability of the region. The same can be said for language, religion, industry, art, commerce, folklore, dress, nutrition, anthropologically determined physical type, and so forth. When we possess these data, we will know more about our necessities, aspirations, deficiencies, and qualities. Knowing the causes of our national problems, we can seek the betterment of the diverse ethnic groups that form the population.

The Constitution of 1857 is of foreign origin, form, and content. It is relevant to the material and intellectual life of the 20 percent of the population that shares European blood and civilization. For the rest, said constitution is exotic and inappropriate. It is wrong to want the same law to rule the urbane citizen of Mexico City and the Lacandón of Chiapas, who roams naked and lives from hunting and fishing in a savage region, having no larger sense of *patria* than what is bounded by his mountains, his women, and his children. And the same law that rules the Lacandón cannot rule the border people of the north, who share the language, industry, commercial aptitudes, and other characteristics of the North American people. Nor is it right that the same law that rules the conservative individual of the high mesas rules also the liberal and innovative people of the coast and the people who live along our southern border, whose culture is more Central American than Mexican. This law is inadequate for the Indians in general, who are mostly illiterate, who speak distinct languages, and who live in different climates. Nor can the same law rule a self-made, industrious man of progressive tendencies and the aristocrat who was educated abroad and returns home with a repulsive hybridism of customs and ideas.

When a ruler knows the characteristics of the individuals and groups that make up our population, the task of legislating over social life becomes possible. Such legislation requires a broadly defined general constitution and specific laws that are adequate for the ethnico-social and economic characteristics of our different social groups and the geographical conditions of their respective regions. We believe that any government that truly wants to be efficient and nationalistic must promote the acquisition of correct statistical data by any means possible, so that it can know about the population qualitatively as well as quantitatively.

8

Some Considerations on Statistics

First, statistics is a conjunction of qualitative and quantitative data that refer to the population and to its activities at home and abroad.

Second, these data should be systematically and empirically collected so that they have legitimate value and do not falsify the result of calculations that will later be made with them.

Third, mathematical procedures are applied such that comparisons, sums, and correlations can be drawn from these data. Groups, classes, and series will be formed. Maximums and minimums will be obtained, as well as averages, medians, and percentages and so forth. This will be expressed graphically through diagrams when necessary.

Fourth, when these data are observed by persons of real competence, the probable causes of certain unfavorable social phenomena can be deduced and means can be suggested by which these phenomena can be turned into favorable ones. In this way, it is possible to promote the physical, intellectual, and economic development of the population.

Given these general guidelines, which are universally accepted in regard to statistical studies, we will evaluate the positive value of works of statistics already conducted in Mexico and speak of some innovations that could be implemented in order to obtain truly practical results in the future.

A. WORKS OF STATISTICS UNDERTAKEN IN MEXICO

An integrated work of statistics has never been done in Mexico. That is, we have never synthesized data on all of the population of the republic nor have we gathered data on all of their relevant characteristics and activities. With few exceptions, the compilation of data has been conducted naïvely, without scientific systematicity. Only on very few occasions were the mathematical procedures necessary for the management of said data and the deduction of consequent results used. Because of this, the positive value of these studies is limited, and the conclusions that can be drawn from them lack exactitude. In the past, the institutions charged with gathering statistical data were content to produce purely descriptive results. They did not make a practical application of these conclusions, which made it impossible to deduce a means of promoting greater efficiency in the activities of the population.

Deficient works of statistics that have been conducted in our country include those concerned with labor and with the sales prices of certain articles. Ethnico-demographic statistics are of primary importance in countries like Mexico, where the population is heterogeneous in race, culture, language, and nutrition. However, such studies have never produced data of interest or reliable conclusions here. Studies of vital statistics, or the rise or decline of the number of births, deaths, and marriages, have been so limited that their results cannot be summarized. But despite the aforementioned deficiencies, the statistical material already collected by state and federal offices could still yield a great deal of useful data, if this material is properly selected and synthesized.

B. A NATIONALISTIC SENSIBILITY IS NEEDED FOR THE FORMATION OF THE FUTURE MEXICAN STATISTICS

The general concepts used in conducting statistical investigations are the same in all countries, given that the fundamental nature of all men is the same. Nevertheless, one should not and cannot use the same statistical methods or get the same results in all countries. First, in Mexico it would currently be impossible to use the same statistical methods employed in the United States, because we do not count with the powerful economic resources that are necessary for such a task. We also lack competent personnel and the cooperation of a large part of the population, which has always shown itself unwilling to provide data. Second, in Germany and France, ethnographic research is not given a major role in statistical work. Given the unity of those populations in terms of race, culture, and language, other elements of statistics are privileged. Given

the ethnic heterogeneity of the Mexican population, the diversity of its ideals, languages, and so forth, it becomes indispensable to have an ethnographic
reconnaissance and classification of its diverse social groups. This is the only
way of making their characteristics and activities collaborate in a harmonious
national development, so that, in the future, the state of social cohesion that is
inherent in all defined and conscious nationalities can emerge.

Third, studies of the vital statistics of those countries whose nutrition is
based on wheat have established the amount of exertion that is necessary for
a healthy man to generate a normal amount of labor. In Mexico, the results
of similar tests would be different. Differences in the physical environment,
nutrition, and ethnic types influence our own potential for labor. Indigenous
races whose nutrition is based on maize yield a normal degree of work, but
their scarce musculature does not theoretically correspond to that output.
This makes their endurance all the more notable, and something that must be
accounted for in the relevant statistical calculi.

In conclusion, the examples cited in this chapter demonstrate how the
work of statistics that remains to be done in Mexico must rest on general bases
of universal application, but that these should be adapted to the particular
social, biological, and ethnic conditions that characterize our population.

9

The Work of Art in Mexico

It seems risky to classify all of the manifestations of art that exist in Mexico—architecture, sculpture, painting, ceramics, pottery, decorative arts, and so forth. Besides being diverse and little-studied, these art forms differ in terms of their cultural origin, character, technique, and symbolic value. But by having a basic knowledge of the characteristics of Western art, examining the art of the pre-Hispanic period, and studying how the two have influenced each other, one can make the following provisional classification:

1) The work of pre-Hispanic art;

2) The foreign work of art;

3) The work of traditional art that emerged through evolutionary incorporation and the work of traditional art that emerged through systematic incorporation;

4) The work of art of reappearance, by copy; the work of art of spontaneous reappearance.

A. THE WORK OF PRE-HISPANIC ART

This type of art was produced in Mexico until the arrival of the Conquest. Its most interesting manifestations, when compared with objects of the same antiquity in the Orient and Occident, included architecture, feather art, lapidary art, artistic metallurgy of gold and copper, ceramics, profuse and original

48

decoration. Distinctive architectural elements included the corbelled arch, the plastering and polishing of walls and floors, and mural painting. There was also a pavement made of superimposed coats of a concrete made from pumice, conglomerates, and lime. The pre-Hispanic architects employed a column made with a base, shaft, and capital and a prismatic pillar with pyramidal base. All of these artistic and technical achievements can be considered along with a thousand other details that the brevity of this article forces us to omit. Overall, they denote great powers of observation and constructive knowledge among the pre-Hispanic architects, as well as the aesthetic sense that can be observed in the marvelous decorations of their buildings. The same can be said of their gold and silver jewelry, smelted, beaten, and "braided," and the opulent mosaics of feathers, turquoise, rock crystal, and jade. This type of art was produced by the civilizations of the Maya, Aztecs, Teotihuacanos, and Mixteco-Zapotec, and others.

B. THE FOREIGN WORK OF ART

This art has been imported from other countries since the Conquest. It has been slightly influenced by the particular environmental conditions of Mexico, but not by indigenous art. During the sixteenth century, Spanish art predominated, although there were also some traces of the art of Flanders and Italy, given the contact in Europe between Spain, Italy, and the Low Countries. Afterward, the importation of artistic forms was extended to other countries, primarily France. Today, we have art from all of the cultured countries of the world.

C. THE TRADITIONAL WORK OF ART

This is the national work of art, the one that most interests us. As we have said, it has emerged in two ways.

1. *By Evolutionary Incorporation.* This kind of art originated with the Conquest. Spanish and pre-Hispanic art met face-to-face; they invaded one another, mixed, and in many cases melded harmoniously. Looking carefully at manifestations of this kind of art, one can see that they have two clearly defined social sources or bases. The Indian, a living repository of pre-Hispanic art, continued to cultivate it with fervor but was often forced or chose to include elements of Spanish art into his own. The indigenous artistic industries that one finds today are examples of this phenomenon. In the same way, the Spanish promoted and imposed their invasive art but could not prevent elements of pre-Hispanic art from being incorporated into it. This can be seen primarily in architecture. The arches of Tecamachalco and the churches of Coyoacán, Atzcapotzalco, Tlalnepantla, and other colonial towns have a profusion of decorative elements such as flowers, birds, feathers, and geometric motifs that can also be found in the codices and architectural, sculptural, and ceramic monuments of the pre-Hispanic period.

2. *By Systematic Incorporation.* We have said that the kinds of traditional art that emerged from evolutionary incorporation have two sources or bases, the indigenous and the European. Differences between these two sources reflect the distinct sensibilities of the Mexican social classes, which are inclined toward one or the other type of art. The indigenous class keeps and cultivates pre-Hispanic art, reformed by the European. The middle class keeps and cultivates European art, reformed by the indigenous or pre-Hispanic. The so-called aristocratic class claims that its art is purely European.

The passage of time and the economic betterment of the indigenous class will contribute to the ethnic fusion of the population and will also contribute to the fusion of the cultural forms and aesthetic sensibilities of the two principal classes. It is indispensable that we work toward this end. We should systematize the artistic production of the Indian and the middle class as far as our methods and materials allow us. We must bring the former closer to European art and the latter closer to indigenous art. Each group must know the historical antecedents of the art form to which it feels the closest affinity and of that into which it is being incorporated. It is clear that the middle class must first initiate itself in the techniques and character of pre-Hispanic and contemporary indigenous art, given that its members have far more resources with which to illustrate themselves than the Indians presently do. When the middle-class individual and the indigene have the same sensibility in art, we will be redeemed culturally. A national art form, which is one of the great bases of nationalism, will have emerged. Happily, this task is already being undertaken by official and private institutions.

D. THE WORK OF ART OF REAPPEARANCE

1. *By copy.* This consists of older styles of art that are reproduced and faithfully copied in our day, including reproductions of works of pre-Hispanic art and copies of foreign art.

2. *Spontaneous*. This kind of artistic production appears to be the result of a little-known and obscure phenomenon that has often been noted in the art that appeared immediately before the Conquest. There were certain artistic forms that disappeared with the Teotihuacán civilization that flourished in the Valley of Mexico more than ten centuries ago and that are not at all evident among civilizations considered to be Teotihuacán's successors. Some of these forms reappeared, rather mysteriously, around the time of the Conquest. Do two identical artistic forms that appear in the same place but are separated by an interval of more than a thousand years develop for distinct reasons? Or does the later art form originate from the first? Does it develop out of it, even if there does not appear to have been a single link in the long period that separates them? In order to better understand this phenomenon, it is essential that we study the two art forms in question more closely.

10

The Concept of Pre-Hispanic Art

A. THE WESTERN AESTHETIC SENSIBILITY[1]

Works of art that are unearthed by archaeologists are often qualified as aesthetic or anti-aesthetic. But why they are thus qualified is almost never explained. Archaeological[2] art is judged subjectively, as each person thinks that it should be, and not as it is. It is prejudged, not judged, since we have not developed a real sensibility toward the archaeological work of art.

What is artistic about pre-Hispanic artistic productions? Does an archaeological sample cease to be artistic because of the simple fact that it does not inspire us toward an aesthetic emotion that is equal to that inspired by a Classical or modern artwork? It is doubtless that, given how ignorant we are of pre-Hispanic history, these objects do not appear artistic according to our aesthetic sense. Still, there is no logical reason why this art should be denied the artistic character that it had for earlier peoples. We should also ask ourselves why it is that some archaeological productions seem artistic to us and others do not, even if all of them possessed an artistic character when they were created.

No people is devoid of, or especially favored, by artistic impulses. Art exists in all latitudes and in all hearts; its diverse modes and aspects reflect different ways of experiencing and expressing art among diverse human groups. We men of contemporary Western civilization share a way of experiencing and possess-

---

[1] We refer to the European.

[2] In this article, the word "archaeological" is equivalent to prehistory.

ing art; we have a common "pattern of aesthetics." A Latin, a Saxon, a Slav would generally have been in agreement with us when we say, "This is beautiful, artistic." Behind all three of us, there are 3,000 to 5,000 years of previous schools of art that unify our aesthetic sensibilities. We can be thoughtful critics of today's art and of all of the things that were created by Western civilization in the past. Although an impressionist bust by Rodin represents a different chapter in the history of art from a serene Classical bust of Antinous or a stylized face from Medieval Christian art, all three awaken the aesthetic emotion in us. We understand Rodin because we live with him. We understand the art of past times, of Greece, of Rome, of Byzantium, because history, literature, the museum, and other educational factors have permitted us to live with those peoples. We can live their lives, embrace their preferences and aversions, suffer their pains, enjoy their pleasures, and spend time in their environments.

We are prepared to understand and be well-disposed toward this kind of art. In any given moment, our soul can be Hellenic, Roman, or Byzantine and our artistic emotions will always vibrate to the same diapason as men from those times and countries. What we have said about the Romans, Greeks, and Byzantines could also be applied to the other ancestors of Western art: Egypt, Chaldea, Assyria, Phoenicia, Judea, Arabia, India, Persia, and Asia Minor.

To summarize, it can be said that the mental states that preside over the production and contemplation of a work of art stem in large part from the physical-biological and social environment in which said artwork appeared, or from the historical antecedents of the people who produced it. We therefore ask, Can one experience artistic emotions by viewing objects of pre-Hispanic art for the first time? This is logically impossible, since it is impossible to evaluate something of which one has no knowledge. Something that is contemplated for the first time cannot be appreciated or esteemed enough for one to rate it. This is also psychologically impossible, because the mental states produced by the presence of any manifestation of art are the fruit of experience and not spontaneous.

B. EXPERIMENTAL CONCLUSIONS

In order to obtain empirical data on this subject, we showed different examples of pre-Hispanic art to observers who had a good knowledge of Western art but who were ignorant of pre-Columbian civilizations. The observers stated which of these objects they considered artistic and which they considered indifferently or even found repulsive. Then, the following groupings were made. First, the archaeological productions that did not appear artistic to Western sensibilities were grouped together (Plates 1 and 2). Second, the productions that did seem artistic to them were grouped together (Plates 3, 4, and 5). Why was there this difference in evaluations if the manifestations of pre-Hispanic art represented in both groups were unknown to said observers beforehand and were all considered artistic according to pre-Hispanic sensibilities?

1. *Archaeological Production That Does Not Appear Artistic to Western Sensibilities*. The works of art in the first group could not have inspired an aesthetic emotion in the observers. This would be logically and psychologically impossible, given that these objects were previously unknown to them. But for those who know how and why these art forms developed, they are as artistic as those of any country and time.

Let us consider the Aztec figures in Plates 1 and 2 as an example. Given what we know about that civilization, we can cite some of the principal characteristics of its individuals as religious fanaticism, activeness, a warlike spirit, and nomadism. These are things that inspired hatred and provoked persecutions from the other indigenous families that they stumbled across on their long migrations. The high plateaus that they crossed during these millennial pilgrimages were generally sterile and inhospitable. The only other inhabitants were spiny plants and a fauna that consisted of felines, reptiles, and other frightful animals. The horizon was fringed by mountain ranges with jagged and broken profiles or by the zigzag of high-peaked conifer forests. Only the heavens seemed to offer any light. This physical-biological and social setting is expressed with very lively contours in the art and mythology of the ancient Mexicans. These geographic and biological antecedents explain why their major gods were those of war and water, the antithetical symbols of their two eternal enemies: hostile peoples and the sterility of the regions through which they traveled. This is also why their rituals were bloody and macabre and why the lines, surfaces, colors, and decoration of their art are almost devoid of any sense of tranquility or well-being. Where one sees great serenity in the art of Teotihuacán, that of the Aztecs reflects the difficult and chancy life of those who, unable to find sustenance in the rough and sterile regions where they lived, had to conquer and take it by force from others.

2. *Archaeological Production That Appears Artistic to Western Sensibilities*. We can make the a priori assumption that the aesthetic emotion experienced by the observers before the second group of pre-Hispanic artworks

PLATE 1

Aztec art. (*a*) National Museum; (*b*) National Museum; (*c*) National Museum; (*d*) Codex Fejevary-Mayer.

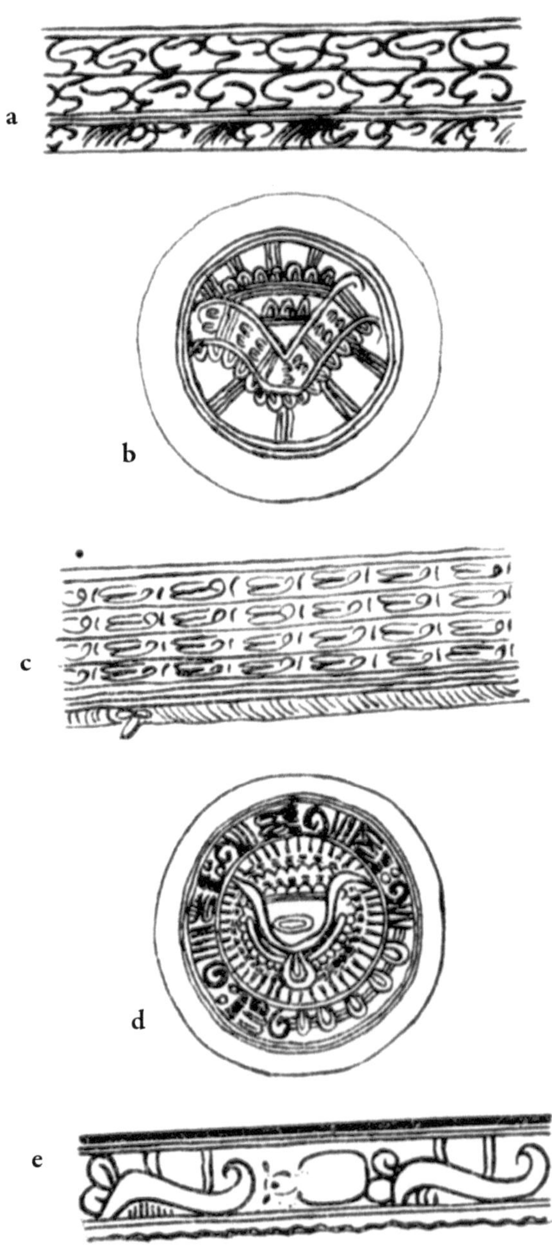

PLATE 2

Pre-Hispanic (Aztec civilization). (*a–e*) Culhuacán. *Album of the International School of American Archaeology and Ethnology*, plates 1, 14, 16, and 23.

(Plates 3, 4, and 5) is logically and psychologically impossible, given that these are as unknown to them as the artworks that were placed in the first group. We can offer two possibilities to explain this apparent paradox.

3. *The First Possibility*. The representations in Plates 3, 4, and 5 appear artistic to the observers because they have morphological resemblance to certain representations in Western art that are familiar to them. These are representations that they are more accustomed to judge, evaluate, produce, and experience. Compare the representations in Plates 3, 4, and 5, which are all pre-Hispanic, with those in Plates 3 bis, 4 bis, and 5 bis, which are all works of Western art. The objects in the first series are agreeable, seem artistic, and awaken emotions in observers with Western sensibilities because, even if they are unfamiliar, they resemble or have a morphological similarity to familiar pieces in the second series. The objects in the first series, like those in the second series, conform to what psychologists call "generic images" in the minds of observers.

4. *The Second Possibility*. It is neither logical, nor psychological, that the observers should experience the same aesthetic emotion when they contemplate the representations in Plates 3, 4, and 5 as when they contemplate those in 3 bis, 4 bis, and 5 bis. Even if they are morphologically similar, these manifestations of art originated in very different physical-biological and social contexts. The mental states that presided over their manufacture were very different.

Let us look at the example of the Aztec head represented in Plate 5, which is generally known as the "Eagle Knight." Given the first possibility described above, it is logical and psychological that the head awakens an aesthetic emotion in the observers, because its appearance suddenly brings Classical art to mind. It contributes to the formation of one of the generic images that we have referred to before. They experience the same aesthetic emotion when they view the Eagle Knight that they would while contemplating the head in Plate 5 bis, which is actually a production of Classical art.

In our opinion, it is neither logical nor psychological to experience such an emotion when contemplating the Eagle Knight, as it was not sculpted beneath the sky of Argolido, or on a Roman campaign, but on the high Mexican plateaus. It was not made by the inspiration of the Greek and Roman soul, but by the Aztec. The aesthetic emotion that we experience when we view it is a psychological fraud. It is hybrid, given that it originates from the contemplation of American forms and the evocation of European ideas.

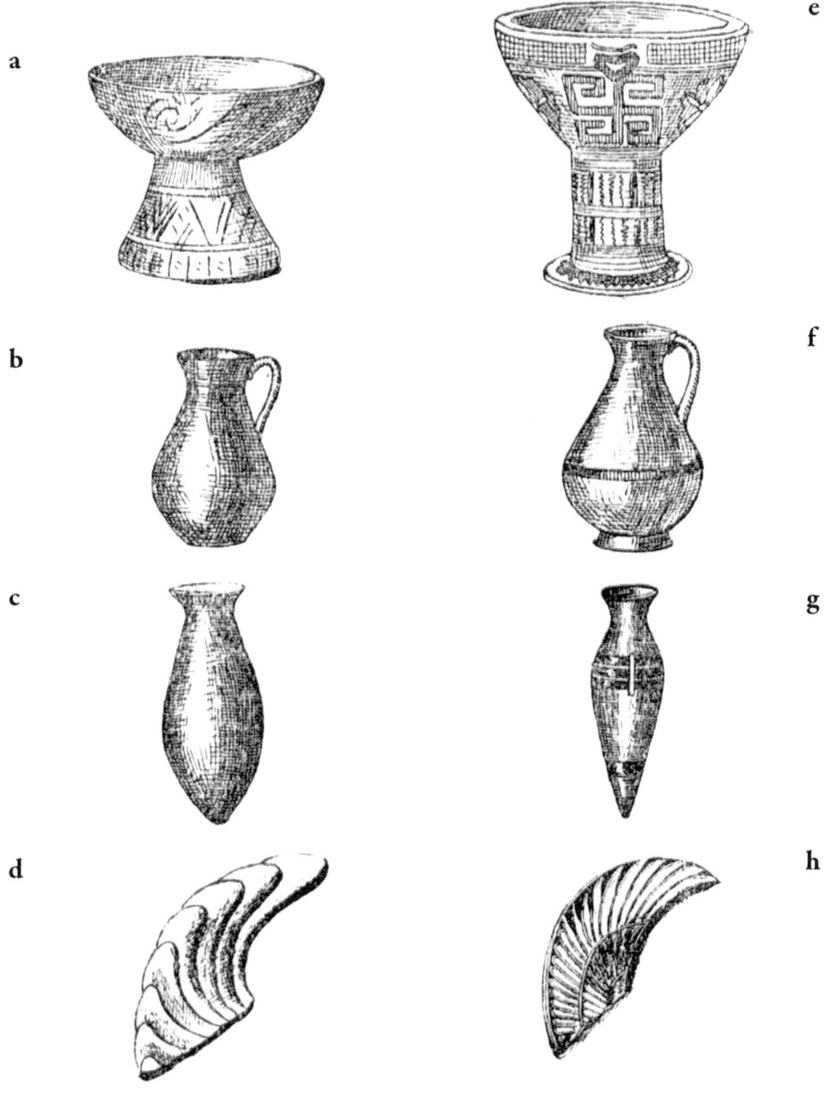

PLATE 3

Pre-Hispanic art. (*a*) National Museum; (*b*) Teotihuacán, Local Museum; (*c*) Teotihuacán, Local Museum; (*d*) Teotihuacán, Local Museum.
Occidental art. (*e*) Phoenician, Perrot and Chipiez, *Historia del Arte*, vol. 3, p. 215; (*f*) Caldean, Perrot and Chipiez, *Historia del Arte*, vol. 2, p. 711; (*g*) Roman, Duruy, *History of the Romans*, vol. 2, p. 413; (*h*) Egypt, Perrot and Chipiez, *Historia del Arte*, vol. 3, p. 832.

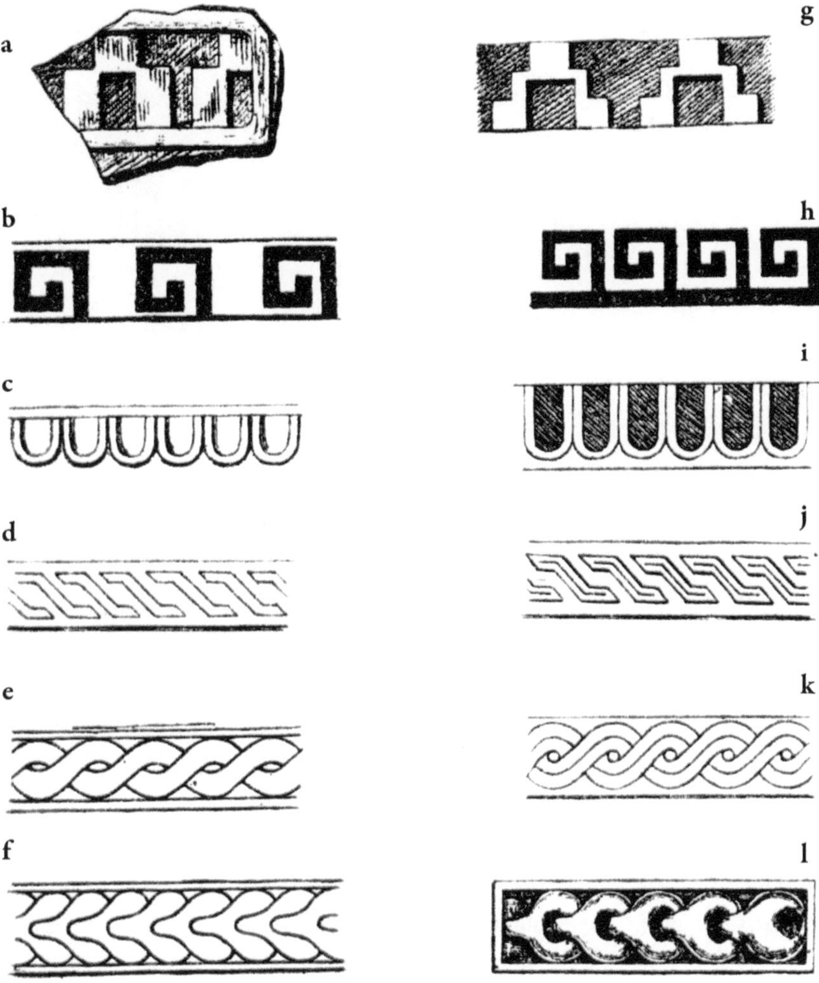

PLATE 4

Pre-Hispanic art. (*a*) Teotihuacán, Local Museum; (*b*) Peñafiel, Monumentos del Arte Mexicano, plate 20; (*c*) Aztec Calendar, National Museum; (*d*) Azcapotzalco, Peñafiel, *Monumentos del Arte Mexicano*, plate 21; (*e*) Peñafiel, *Monumentos del Arte Mexicano*, Plate 17; (*f*) Peñafiel, *Monumentos del Arte Mexicano*, plate 16.
Occidental art. (*g*) Persia (Persepolis), Perrot and Chipiez, *Historia del Arte*, vol. 5, p. 531; (*h*) Chaldea, Perrot and Chipiez, *Historia del Arte*, vol. 2, p. 132; (*i*) Phoenicia, Perrot and Chipiez, *Historia del Arte*, vol. 3, p. 810; (*j*) Archaic Greece, Perrot and Chipiez, *Historia del Arte*, vol. 7, p. 148; (*k*) Phoenicia, Perrot and Chipiez, *Historia del Arte*, vol. 3, p. 810; (*l*) Contemporary decoration, drawing by Promeda.

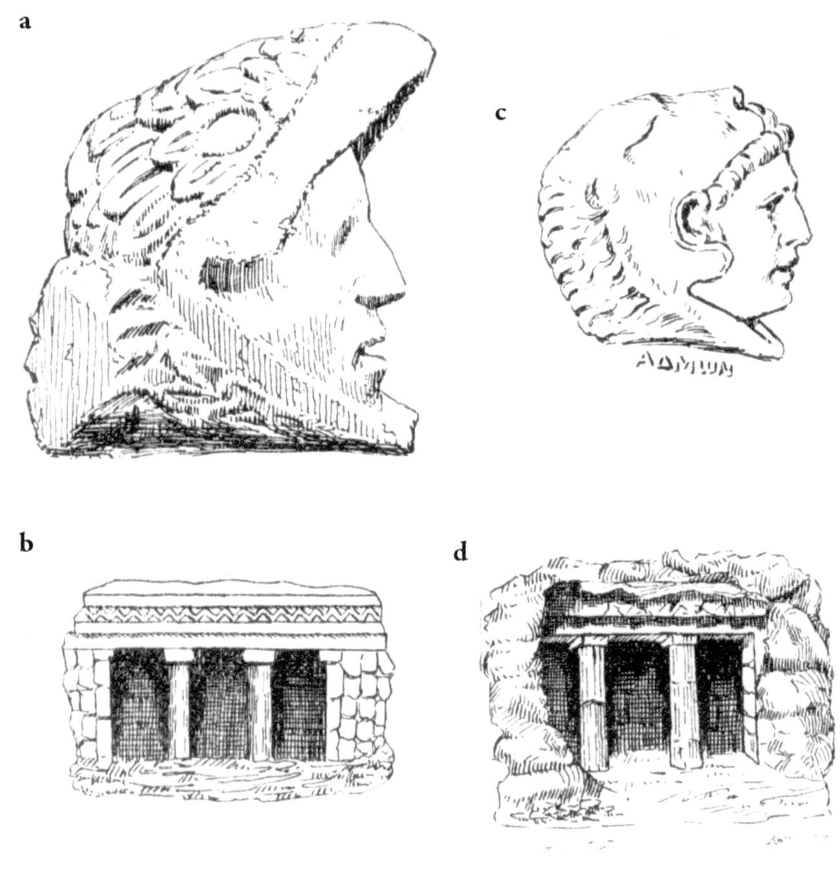

PLATE 5

Pre-Hispanic art. (*a*) Eagle Knight, National Museum, Mexico; (*b*) Uxmal, Yucatán. *Occidental art.* (*c*) Admon (323 to 336 B.C.), "Tressor Numimastique ed de gliptique," plate XIII; (*d*) Egypt, Perrot and Chipiez, *Historia del Arte*, vol. 1, p.256.

5. *The True Point of View.* In order for the head of the Eagle Knight to inspire in us the deep, legitimate, and proper aesthetic emotion that the contemplation of art should make one feel, it is necessary for there to be harmony between its material form and how we experience it. The term "Eagle Knight" is deceptive and unexpressive. We should know when and where he lived and the hows and whys of his life. The Eagle Knight is not a discobolos or a Roman gladiator. He represents the inscrutability, the fierceness, the serenity of an Aztec warrior from the noble classes. The sculptor who made his likeness was familiar with the age in which he lived, was a witness to his combats, to his defeats and triumphs, and to all of those epic visions that appeared in his mind. One sees in him the immutability, the repose, in which Indian faces appear to dream through pleasure or pain. One sees in him the cruel pride of the sons of Mexico, the metropolis of her time, who was lady and mistress over a thousand bloodstained territories. One sees in him the abstract ideas that dominated that age of bloody religious rites and voluntary tortures, of endless and obsessive reflections on death, of mysterious cosmogonies.

Only in this way, knowing all of its historical antecedents, can we feel pre-Hispanic art. Otherwise, our judgment of this art will be disoriented, and contemporary productions made with pre-Hispanic motifs will suffer from a vacuous hybridism.

II

Art and Science in the Period of Independence

Our historians have conducted nuanced investigations regarding the social and economic innovations that followed independence from Spain. But little attention has been paid to other innovations of artistic and scientific character that took place during the same period. In the Colonial period, the Mexican population of Spanish origin was similar to the people of Spain in most respects. In Mexico as in Spain, art had attained an evolutionary development that was far in advance of the scientific knowledge of the same period. A profusion of anonymous artists existed for every Hernandez or Alzate[1] who made his sporadic contributions to scientific knowledge. Silently and patiently, they created that lofty and extensive work of beauty that is our colonial art.

By the turn of the eighteenth century, activities that contributed to the production of the beautiful enjoyed complete supremacy over scientific research. Our colonial architecture had reached such an interesting development that even the extravagant descriptions of Humboldt do not exaggerate its beauty. Even miserable villages that were lost in the mountains or buried in the valleys, and that were home to fewer than a hundred souls, had beautiful buildings crowned by the brilliant polychromy of high tiled domes and the filigreed stone of statues and crosses. The Romanesque, the Plateresque, the Baroque, the Churrigueresque, the Mudejar, the Classical, all lofty styles that contrib-

---

[1] Francisco Hernandez de Toledo (1514–1587), physician and botanist; José Antonio de Alzate y Ramirez (1737–1799), priest, naturalist, astronomer, and antiquarian.—Trans.

uted a typical unique aspect to our art. American sensibilities and historical antecedents imposed forms onto these styles that made them distinct from the European original. Besides the purely aesthetic concerns, this architecture adapted European forms to regional climatic conditions, such as high ceilings, ample corridors, spacious courtyards, floors of tile and brick, and so forth.

Science, on the other hand, stagnated during the Colonial period. The exaggerated Catholicism of the age and the fear of repression from the metropole smothered the lights of knowledge that would later inspire the desire for independence. Because of this, the scientific advances of Europe were unknown in America. To see this, one must simply glance at the bibliography of sixteenth-, seventeenth-, and eighteenth-century Mexico. The vast majority of these works represent theology, literary writing, and history, with almost nothing written that was truly scientific in character.

When independence was achieved, a curious phenomenon took place. The emancipation of the country produced a general artistic stagnation and paralyzed certain manifestations of colonial art. At the same time, scientific knowledge was greatly disseminated. What were the works of art produced in Mexico during the nineteenth century? Did artworks reflect aesthetic tendencies that represented the mentality and way of life of the population, as was the case with colonial art? Although some of our typical art forms continued to be produced after independence, others changed in character and no longer demonstrated the cultural fusion that is necessary for the creation of a truly national tradition in Mexico. Architecture, for example, gradually lost its colonial stamp. European- and North American–style buildings supplanted the beautiful and more appropriate constructions of past centuries. Exotic styles were copied in a servile manner; styles of constructions more adequate for other climates were imposed on our soil. As a result, the Mexican architecture of the nineteenth century lacks a typical character or style. Its hybridism is so pronounced that it has never earned a denomination that would distinguish it from the periods that came before or those that are yet to come. This deplorable architectural cosmopolitanism has become even worse in the first decades of the twentieth century. In the newer neighborhoods, one finds ten exotic buildings of detestably bad taste for every one that is truly beautiful and adequate for our climate. Ridiculous xenophiles say that when they travel down the paved streets of those aristocratic places, they are reminded of identical corners in European and North American cities. This is a false assertion, as the heterogeneous collection of poorly copied and interpreted buildings in modern Mexico cannot be compared, either in style or in disposition, to those cities. In those cities, styles that are exotic in Mexico are typical and authentic, the fruit of a natural artistic process, and not artificially imposed, poorly reproduced, and inappropriate.

Other manifestations of our artistic culture conserved their typical character, but they were isolated and ceased to contribute to the emergence of a national art. These include embroidery, weaving, ceramics, and many others. By the end of the Colonial period, indigenous art and Spanish art were melding so harmoniously that the resulting mixed art form was being produced and used profusely by both races. But during the nineteenth century, European artistic ideas were imported, and indigenous art came to be cultivated by the indigenous race alone. The rest of the population degenerated in its aesthetic sensibility, which is now nothing more than a poor imitation of the European.

In contrast to this decadence of art, scientific research and knowledge began to flower after independence. The revolution that made France the standard-bearer of science was reflected even in Mexico. New books and periodicals were received, new forms of scientific speculation were adopted, and young Mexicans went to that nation to be educated, bringing brilliant lights back with them. Because of this, it has been said that the Mexican science of the past century was the legitimate daughter of French science, whereas our colonial art was born of our own soil.

12

· ·

Department of Fine Arts

In Mexico today, there are a great many directorates and institutes: the Department of Public Works, the Geological Institute, the Medical Institute, and so on and so on. There is not, however, a Department of Fine Arts. If it is well and good that special institutions exist for the cultivation of the sciences, is it not logical that art should also have its altars or worshippers in Mexico?

In almost all countries, art offers the supreme expression and ultimate essence of human activities. The same does not happen in Mexico. In this marvelous country, where we all believe ourselves to be touched by the artistic madness, there is almost no artistic production. Anarchy and aesthetic chauvinism rule. Among us, there are impeccable Hellenists who live with and truly experience Homer, who only appreciate the Classical forms and rhythmic proportions of the Parthenon, who only comprehend the serene figures of Phidias. Others commune with the aesthetic credo of the Renaissance. Others admire the beauty of colonial art. There are those who are moved aesthetically by viewing the creations of pre-Hispanic artists. We also have cubists, divisionists, futurists, and other poorly understood "exoticists" incorporated into our Mexican artistic scene.

What has this situation, which could be called a true divisionism, produced? Today, there is not a single artist or lover of art in Mexico who can understand another. One takes the smooth and marvelous Greek sculpture to be his standard, the other a smiling Donatello, the other a stylized Eagle Knight, and the "exoticist" a pyramid that he says is a smiling Madonna. Amidst such disorientation, the essence of true art, which is equally present

65

in the Greek sculpture, the Donatello, the Eagle Knight, and the Madonna, is misunderstood and miscommunicated. Amidst such confusion, Mexicans do not produce legitimate works of art, because legitimate art would have to be of a local and national character. It should represent, intensify, and beautify the joys, the pains, the life, and the soul of a people. This will not happen so long as those who are in charge of making art—painters, sculptors, musicians, authors—walk down divergent paths and promote exclusivist sensibilities.

The personality of the true artist is supported by two basic principles. First, an ample and unprejudiced understanding of the art that he cultivates, be this the harmony of words, of form, of color, or of sound. This includes a historical and experiential knowledge of its origin, character, evolution, and contemporary tendencies. Second, an artist must have an integral education in all of the Fine Arts, including painting, sculpture, literature, and music. This knowledge must be acquired and carefully developed. The other psychic aptitudes and physiological conditions of the artist cannot be acquired or formed; one must be born with them.

At the risk of offending overwrought patriotism, we recognize that there has not been a Velásquez, Wagner, Rodin, or Anatole France in Mexico in the four centuries of our Europeanized intellectual life. It is probable that such men will not appear so long as we continue to dedicate ourselves to foreign modalities of art rather than to our own. We should remain without prejudice against learning about these foreign art forms. Nevertheless, we should never compete with foreign artists to produce foreign art, as we will only make fools of ourselves.

It should be said that the Department of Fine Arts does not *pretend to create art*, as has been said maliciously, but promotes an environment that is propitious for the spontaneous emergence of a national art form. To this end, it will provide material and intellectual support for artists, stimulating their production and making a wide and unified aesthetic community available to them.

13

There Is No Prehistory!

Such an affirmation can be made unequivocally, without fear of being contradicted. There has been no lack of hypotheses about the existence of prehistoric man in Mexico. Peñon Man, Tequixquiac Man, Chapala Man, and who knows how many other fabulous men have been proposed for intellectual debate. But a scientific naïveté that was forgivable a quarter-century ago is inadmissible and ridiculous today.

Fortunately, the sin was not ours alone. Many researchers insisted until recently that there was a prehistoric American man. The most famous among them, Ameghino,[1] dedicated the greater part of his life to demonstrating the presence of that ancient man in the Argentine pampas. Hrdlička,[2] the most learned among the opponents of such a theory, has used the strictest scientific method and consulted all of the investigations undertaken to date to deduce that American man is not prehistoric but contemporary or modern. This hypothesis is supported by the geological context of American man. We will cite some proofs.

A. PREHISTORIC ART

The first three great periods of sedimentary formation—the Primary, Secondary, and Tertiary—are similar on all continents, except for a few variations.

------

[1] Florentino Ameghino (1854–1911).—Trans.
[2] Aleš Hrdlička (1869–1943).—Trans.

However, the Quaternary period presents notable differences in Europe and America, particularly as regards the men and the animals that lived in that remote time. The Quaternary fauna of Europe was characterized by horses, bison, elephants larger than those of today, carnivorous bears the size of oxen, hippopotami, reindeer, two-horned rhinoceros, and so forth. The American fauna of the period was characterized by gigantic llamas, Megatherium, and huge-carapaced glyptodonts that looked like giant tortoises. The bones and plaster reproductions of the latter two can be seen in our National History Museum. The fact that man had already appeared in Europe when this ancient fauna existed has been proved in several ways, including the paintings of those animals that have been found in the great prehistoric caves of Spain and France. These could not have been made later, as these animals all disappeared or retreated to arctic regions, as the reindeer and wolverine have done. In Mexico and in America in general, man did not appear in the company of the Quaternary fauna. The first men appeared hundreds of centuries later when these animals had already disappeared. No sculptures or rock paintings of that ancient fauna have been found in America to date.

B. ANTHROPOMETRIC CHARACTERISTICS

The form and capacity of the cranium and the form of the maxillae, teeth, and other parts of the skeleton of prehistoric man differ greatly from the corresponding parts in the skeleton of contemporary Europeans and from the corresponding parts of both contemporary and ancient Americans. The skeletons of contemporary and ancient Americans, however, do not differ from each other significantly. No skeletons of what could be called prehistoric man have been found in the Americas.

C. UNSUSTAINABILITY OF THE INDUSTRIAL CLASSIFICATION

Quaternary times in Europe can be divided into periods marked by characteristic industries: the Age of Chipped Stone, the Age of Polished Stone, the Bronze Age, and the Iron Age. The American man of the sixteenth century used and produced chipped stone, polished stone, and copper but ignored the use of iron. This particular situation does not permit one to advance any conclusions derived by classifying the antiquity of American man in terms of industry.

D. PROVENIENCE OF THE AMERICAN

Recent investigations presented in the Second Pan-American Scientific Congress demonstrated that the settlers of America came from Asia, definitively dispelling the theory of a prehistoric American man. Now then, if there were no prehistoric men in America, and therefore in Mexico, why do we insist on referring to the times before the Conquest as prehistoric? The only institution in our country that has proscribed the use of the term "prehistoric" in its research on Mexico, in support of a proposition by the author, is the Mexican Academy of History.

14

Synthetic Concept of Archaeology

For some, archaeology is nothing more than a way of passing the time. Archaeological investigations are a way of determining if Moctezuma wore rope or leather sandals on his feet, or of knowing if Cuauhtémoc did his own "manicure" or entrusted this to bronzed "toiletistes." Other wags whisper that archaeologists hunt for a depository of Toltec "unfalsifiables," as they cannot believe that a serious man would find interest in unearthing a bunch of stones with "monkeys" and hieroglyphics on them. There are also those who think that our antiquities should be preserved "just because" or "because they are pretty." Unfortunately, that loss of public esteem is justified by the deeds of many frauds who call themselves archaeologists, with the same justification that they might call themselves pedicurists or astronomers. In archaeology as in good fortune, there have been many who are called but few who are chosen. We must therefore unmask that intellectual rabble that has been destroying and discrediting the monuments of our past.

What is archaeology? The science of the ancient? The study of ancient architectural monuments, of archaic ceramics . . . of indigenous manuscripts? We have heard this question asked a thousand times and answered differently each time. This should give the reader a sense of the conventionalism of this word. For some, it has a definition as broad as the ocean or the earth, and for others it is restricted within ridiculous limits. We will attempt to define the significance that this much-discussed term can have among us. We cannot simply accept the literal significance of archaeology as "the science or study of ancient things." Defined in this way, it would encompass the study of other ancient things, like paleozoology, paleobotany, and so forth.

Archaeology is an integral part of that conjunction of knowledge that is of most interest to all of humanity: anthropology, or the "science of man." Anthropology provides knowledge of peoples in three ways: by physical type, by language, and by their culture or civilization. We consider archaeology to be the study of the culture or civilization of the human groups that inhabited our country before the Conquest.[1] This differs considerably from how people in Europe define the discipline of archaeology, the length of time that it encompasses, and its relationship to prehistory and history.

The archaeological study of pre-Columbian civilization must focus on both its material and intellectual manifestations. The first of these include architecture, ceramics, codices or manuscripts, sculpture, painting, domestic and industrial implements, weapons, and all of the other material objects that are the work of that civilization. The second series of manifestations of pre-Columbian civilization includes ethical and aesthetic ideas, religious concepts, scientific knowledge, and the organization of religious, civil, and military institutions. In general, this second category includes cultural manifestations of abstract character. Knowledge of different aspects of pre-Columbian culture contributes to our understanding of the roots of the characteristics that distinguished the Mexican population during the Colonial period. Knowing these aspects of the past, we can authoritatively approach the study of the current population, a knowledge that should be the true gospel of good government.

We now see how transcendent are the practical ends of archaeology, which go far beyond knowing about the Aztec systems of manicure and the footwear of Moctezuma and Cuahtemoc.

---

[1] The author recently presented to the Mexican Academy of History regarding the true chronological limits of history and archaeology, which we will not transcribe here because of their length.

15

The Values of History

Values of history—it seems to us that history has two values: the speculative and the transcendent. History is essentially the collection of information about the nature, origin, character evolution, and tendencies of past civilizations. When this information exists passively in libraries or in the minds of men, the value of history is only theoretical. But history offers a transcendent value if we think of it as a copious archive, as an inexhaustible fountain of the experiences through which humanity has reached its diverse stages of florescence and decadence. This is especially the case when we use those experiences to improve the well-being of contemporary civilizations. The careful observation and progressive application of these past experiences give us an important perspective on the progress and ascendant march of humanity. This is the case with scientific knowledge, which becomes more extensive and better grounded every day. This said, we cannot overgeneralize about the course of history, as there are many cases in which evolution has not been ascendant, in spite of the influence of previous historical experiences. For example, art and morality ascend and decay through cycles in which the experience of the past is no impediment to the repetition of certain patterns.

The experiences of the past might constitute history in and of themselves, but they remain mute and invisible to us if we do not make an effort to make sense of them, classify them, and present them to the public. In this simple article, it would be tiresome for the reader and difficult for the author to detail all of the aspects that must be accounted for in so difficult a task. Therefore, we will only make reference to three of the most important dimensions that our history offers.

A. THE BASIC ASPECTS OF MEXICAN HISTORY

What are the chronological and geographical limits of our history? What place does it occupy and what function does it play in relation to the other kinds of knowledge? These questions have not been resolved in Mexico. Even though we do not have the vanity to pretend to resolve them satisfactorily, we will present our general ideas, anticipating the justified criticisms and censures that will be made of them.

    1. *Chronological Limits.* We can place the origins of Mexican history in the more or less distant past. Some authors take the point of departure of our history to be thousands of years ago, others write the history of events that took place a few decades ago, and others are sure to write about events that have not yet appeared to the historical perspective. The chronological limits of history vary according to the specific civilization or race being historicized. The point of departure for Mayan chronology—which is itself a form of history—is many centuries in the past. The experiences of the Aztec family of Tenochtitlán take on a historical character in the fourteenth century (when they were represented in the hieroglyphic manuscripts, architecture, and sculpture) and when living Indians gave accounts to the Spanish after the Conquest. On the other hand, there are indigenous groups like the Lacandónes of Chiapas or the Huicholes of Tepic and Jalisco, who have only been known to historians since the last century. Lastly, there are still groups of Mayas in the Mexican Petén that are unknown to us from the historical—or from any other—perspective. Understood in these terms, our history does not begin when the Spanish conquerors appeared on our beaches, as has been proclaimed up until today, but from distinct periods before and after that event.

    2. *Geographical Limits.* The history of Mexico should encompass the social groups that have constituted the population of Mexican territory and indirectly address those foreign peoples that have influenced our way of being or that have been influenced by us. We must consider the population of our current territory and of Central America as far as Panamá (Chiriquí), which is as far as our pre-Columbian influence reached. We must also consider the history of the North American territory that was once a part of Mexico. We must have an indirect account of the past of Spain, the South American republics, the United States, and France, as these nations exercised an important influence on our own history. One must also know something about the history of all of the countries in general, as all countries have exercised a remote or near influence on each other.

3. *Topical Limits.* Many great folio volumes have been written, many Byzantine discussions were begun, the eloquence of brilliant speeches was unleashed, and we still do not know the place of history within the classification of the sciences. Nor do we know what falls within its realm and what does not. We will not contribute a single line to that battle of subtleties. Personally, we think that everything that has existed, tangibly or intangibly, in the material or intellectual world can be documented historically and used for the benefit of the present. If, for example, we are grain merchants, we will be most successful in our business if we understand the history of its principal activities. That way, we can learn about the successes and failures of those who preceded us in that occupation. The relevance of such studies becomes clear if one takes into account the fact that many of the industrial and agricultural successes of modern Germany and other nations are the result of the intensive historical investigation of the relevant activities.

We propose that the content and scope of the history that is taught in our classrooms be expanded and that it not be reduced to rote memorization, which offers little utility to the specialist and depresses the mind of the student. We must also take care that the histories we write be consistent in their methods and ideas. Have we not seen mediocre historians use and confound terms such as "history," "prehistory," and "archaeology"? Do phrases like "philosophy of history" not bubble forth from seemingly authorized lips, with the same impropriety that any man on the street might say "chemistry of history" or "obstetrics of history" rather than "history of philosophy" or "history of chemistry" or "history of obstetrics"?

4. *Integration.* Our history, which should consist of the recompilation of true information concerning all aspects of the Mexican population in all of its evolutionary stages, has been little more than the recompilation of facts about *some* aspects of *some* groups in *some* of their evolutionary stages.

5. *Common Prejudices.* We give preference to the history of the social classes whose civilization is derived from Europe, as if the indigenous classes that are the base of the population were of no importance. Little original research has been conducted on any subject, and what little has been written tends to be tiresome and repetitive. The histories written in our country have tended to be personalist rather than general—presidents, emperors, magnates, and social associations have attracted nearly all of the attention of the historian. The multitudes, whose actions are of prime importance for knowing the development of sociological phenomena, have barely been touched. The activities of religious, political, and military orders have been described and commented upon, although we ignore the history of our plastic art and artists, of our industry and industrialists, of our commerce and our traders, of our agriculture and our agriculturalists.

B. THE AESTHETIC ASPECT

There are histories that are purely descriptive and directed toward instructing the reader agreeably but superficially, while leaving critical questions, appropriate methods, and certified points of view to others. The following is an essay on this aspect of our history that makes no pretense of having literary value, and we confess beforehand it does not.

Mexico, with more titles than any other country of America, boasts a grand past that is attractive not only to the studious man but to whoever loves the environment of mysterious beauty in which the memory of bygone deeds still flourishes. The indigenous tradition, pragmatic, vigorous, and picturesque, allows us to see how the life of the Mexicans was before the Conquest. Their arts seem original and very novel to our aesthetic sensibilities. Theirs was an ingenious industry, a complex, strong, and wise social organization. Their religion consisted of strange rituals in which fresh blood, crystalline copal, and blackened rubber were the highest offerings. Theirs was a limitless pantheon that held a place for the creator god and for the 400 gods of wine and drunkenness. The strength of their military institutions surprised the Spanish captains.

These memories revive the defeated race before our eyes. We perceive the glorious city that was a stage for their greatness. We almost feel their coppery skin, hear their war cries. We feel the terror and admiration that the warriors of Cortés felt during the "noche triste," when they found themselves facing a people that knew how to surrender their own lives and how to take those of others. We will also witness the impotent agony of those men who resisted the historic siege of Tenochtitlán for months, when their misery was such that they devoured the insects of the lake, snakes, and even the corpses of those who had already died of starvation. The inevitable surrender comes soon after, and it is described in such detail that we can almost see it. Deities tumble from temples, blunting the narrow steps. The smoke of the ritual braziers no longer twists in capricious volutes. The temple is empty, one can only see a cross standing over everything. In the distance, in the streets and canals, the armor of the victors looks like flashes of fire. Blood, like a royal cloak, reddens a city in its death throes.

Then, Cortés, the invincible warrior who is also an administrator and statesman, continues to conquer, build, and legislate. He throws the first seeds of European civilization on American soil and throws barrels of American gold into the coffers of Castile. Later, the audiencias appear. There, life consists of accusations, intrigues, and calumnies launched to attain some personal benefit. The victor gathers his booty amidst a lake of blood, which is always indigenous blood. Fortunately, alongside the wounds and humiliations, the indigenes receive the great comfort provided by the missionaries.

Already, one sees the fusion. There is a mixing of blood, ideas, and industries, of virtues and vices. The mestizo type emerges with pristine purity, as he represents the first harmonious product of two races. One sees nubile maidens with large dark eyes, straight and very white teeth, and tiny hands and feet that betray their Indian heritage. Others have flowing golden curls that proclaim their Spanish blood. An Arab/Spanish architecture was imposed but executed with the undeniable hand of an Indian worker who remembered the contours and lines of his teocallis and the rich ornamentation of his ancient palaces, jewelry, and textiles. The flowers that appear so frequently in Mudejar architecture are the *xochitl* flowers that appeared in pagan painting and sculpture. On closer examination, the festoons of laurels and acanthus that are sculpted on doorjambs are covered by the feathers that adorned the image of Quetzalcoatl, the mythical "serpent of precious feathers." The Christianity that was preached pleadingly by the missionaries and with manacles and beatings by the soldiers is still not understood by the converts. The Mother of God inspires love and respect in the natives because they see in her the goddess of harvests, the goddess of their waters, the goddess of their loves. Tonantzin has only changed her ritual garments.

The viceroys represented the absolute power of His Catholic Majesty, and many of them were men of high and noble virtue. There was Mendoza, an energetic leader, but a just man and a true Christian. There was Velasco, known as the "father of the Indians," who irritated the peninsular Spaniards because of his love for the subjugated pariahs. However, most of these viceroys were bland, indolent, and egotistical and ignored the oppression of their humblest subjects. The sinister memory of some of these is still reddened by the blood that they spilled.

This is an age of chivalrous legends, of mysterious crimes, of exaggerated mysticism, of sudden fortunes, and of artistic flowering. Some of the Creole aristocracy that emerged are noble in blood, but most are only ennobled by the wealth that the Spanish worshipped. The Creole scarcely tolerates the mestizo and practically ignores the existence of the Indian, except when he is working in his fields or excavating in his mines. Convents appear by the hundreds, and one's view is dotted with blue, white, and black habits. The Holy Inquisition sharpens its claws. Day and night it uses them to pierce flesh that is old and flaccid; firm, sun-tanned, and full of life; or even soft and innocent before the first cries of puberty. There are pathetic little flames burning in every corner, the light of which barely flickers across the face of some miraculous saint and barely illuminates the gaze of the worshippers. The fortunes of this time are fabulous: gold plates for holidays and silver for ordinary days; a profusion of silks, jewels, and precious wines from Europe, China, Japan, and India. Devotion, art, and vanity built sumptuous palaces that aggrandized the capital of the kingdom and rich cathedrals that could never be filled, given their immense size.

After this long national life, independence came with flashes of light and torrents of blood. Everything changed, transformed, was annihilated . . . but was also reborn. New life emerged, evolved, and elevated itself. One could say that independence was a great pyre in which the gaudy jewelry that had decorated the colonial centuries was purified into a stream of brilliant and pure gold with which to make new forms.

The first half of the nineteenth century was not the promised time for Mexico, not the period of fortification and consolidation dreamed and hoped for by the heroic independentists. Tears, pain, and blood flowed everywhere, even though the glorious dream of emancipation was already a tangible reality. Nobody knew where the *patria* was. People fought to live and lived to fight. Our souls became prisoners of an insane disorientation. The loss of half of the nation's territory cost less Mexican blood than was spilled in any of our civil wars. Only the screams of agony heard at Chapultepec and Molino del Rey proclaimed that honor still remained in our nation.[1]

After that terrible drama, the worst tragedy of our history, blood continued to flow, as liberating lights came to dispel the shadows of many past years. The reform and Constitution of 1857 seemed like torches that would always illuminate the path of the *patria*. Unfortunately, the nation's destiny was once again lulled into sleep, silencing the noble impulses that were just beginning to

---

[1] These last two sentences are both references to the Mexican-American War of 1846–1848.—Trans.

take hold. There came an era in which brilliant vestments hid open sores and cancers.

Then came the Revolution of 1910, like a second independence that demolished these decadent structures. Only this time, the pike demolished higher and bored deeper. The history of the revolution is still not complete. We must dedicate ourselves to observe and compile what can be called "living historical material." This is information based not on documents but on the direct and experiential observation of life. Afterward, the history of the revolution can be written.

C. THE OBJECTIVE ASPECT

If one were to ask a blind man about how he senses the world in which he lives, his opinion will differ greatly from that of a man who has always looked upon what surrounds him. He will say that the aesthetic emotion that music produces in him is the deepest. Some oral ideas are more elevated than others. The softness of some bodies is pleasant to his touch, whereas the roughness of others is repulsive. He will consider some foods to be delicious and others detestable. Still, he will not know the beauty of matter, as there is no blue sky for him, no tumultuous ocean, no wooded mountains. He could not be moved by the expressions of pain, of joy, of anger that are seen in the faces of men. His sensibilities are incomplete, his life is fragmented—it is half of a life.

In the same way, we live in a world of historical shadows. We can hardly perceive the picturesque life of the past; our sensibility is poor and incomplete. The evocation of any stage of history is pale, colorless, unexpressive, if we can only reproduce it in an abstract way. To truly live with the past is to experience it face-to-face. We can use the example of the times of Moctezuma II. With indigenous chronicles and manuscripts, it is possible to know the political, mythical, and ethical ideas of that time, and even to know of the different military, religious, civil, and political institutions. Using media like photography, painting, sculpture, architecture, and authentic objects, we can reconstruct models of palaces; the picturesque clothing of monarchs, noble lords, priests, warriors, workers, and slaves; as well as domestic or ritual utensils, scenes, and ceremonies. As we contemplate all of these material representations and learn about the ideas that presided during that period, our knowledge of the past will be complete. The legitimate sensibility and emotions of that period are vigorously and naturally awakened in us, and not artificially and weakly as would happen if we only knew them theoretically. What we have said about pre-Columbian life in Mexico can also be said for the Colonial and independence periods.

What can be done to promote this kind of historical objectivism? We must amplify existing museums and build even more, developing efficient means of display, adequate descriptive classification, and practical guides and catalogs. More importantly, we must begin to write objective history, smudge fewer pages with biased description, and include more illustrations. Most of all, the history that we write must bring us closer to the diverse objects, clothing, architecture, and sculpture preserved in museums and other places.

16

Revision of the Latin American Constitutions

We have noted how the legislative bodies of the future should pay greater attention to the anthropological study of the populations that they govern. In this way, the constitution and general laws of the country can provide the most efficient and authoritative means with which to meet the needs and seek the well-being of the population. This should be the only objective of any constitution. It was also noted that individuals of Indian race, or those in whom that blood predominates, constitute the great majority of the national population. The rest of the population is made up of individuals of European blood, or those who have this in a greater proportion to indigenous blood. Up until now, the constitutions and legislations of independent Mexico had been derived exclusively from the needs of this latter group and have tended to promote its betterment. The Indian population was left in a greater state of abandon by these laws than it had been under the famous Laws of the Indies created by the Spanish monarchy. These colonial laws constituted a powerful barrier against the exploitation of the Indians and forbade the enslavement of the Indian. Even if they were not entirely free, at least the Indians were never slaves in the way that individuals of the black race were. Other colonial laws prohibited the Inquisition from rending the Indians with its claws, as it did the whites. The legal protection of collective landholdings permitted the Indians to cultivate their lands patriarchally and to preserve many aspects of their pre-Hispanic system of land distribution.

If imperialist nations like England, France, and Spain established laws in their colonies that were developed in accordance with the nature and needs of the respective indigenous populations, a democratic and independent government should consider this same problem with even greater care. Taking into account that the same urgent problem is imposed on all of the Latin American nations, the following propositions were submitted for the approval of the Great Executive Commission [of the Pan-American Scientific Congress]. Approval was sought for the resolutions that appear after these propositions.

A. CONSIDERING:

1st—That constitutions and laws are or should be derived from the nature and necessities of the populations that they are meant to govern.

2nd—That the constitutions and laws of almost all of the Latin American countries are a more or less faithful copy of European or North American constitutions and laws. Insofar as this is the case, they are only appropriate for the social element of those countries that is similar to European or North American social elements in terms of its origin, culture, language, or all three.

3rd—That for Latin American nations like Argentina, where the vast majority of the population is composed of European individuals or individuals of European origin, the current constitution might be appropriate. It is adequate to the nature of the population and to its necessities.

4th—That in the numerous Latin American countries that are in the same situation as Mexico, the population that is constituted by indigenous people has remained disarticulated from the national whole. This population remains an obstacle to progress because of its political passivity. Because of this untenable social equilibrium, the Indian cannot or does not want to collaborate as efficiently as he would be capable of. In this case, the constitutions and laws that forcibly rule him restrict his development, as they are exotic and inappropriate for his needs and aspirations.

5th—That even though the United States of North America only counts 250,000 indigenes, its government has actively sought the favorable development of this population by observing and addressing their needs. This can be seen by observing the Indian reservations established in that republic.

B. RESOLUTION:

That the convenience of revising their existing constitutions be suggested to the Latin American republics in which the population of indigenous blood predominates. In this way, their constitutions will respond to the nature and needs of all of the elements that constitute the population, promoting a harmonious and unified development. Through this, the bases of a truly effective Panamericanism can be positively strengthened.

17

Our Laws and Our Legislators

In the previous chapter, we discussed one of the propositions that the Mexican delegation presented before the Second Pan-American Scientific Congress that took place in Washington, D.C., which was the convenience of revising and reforming the constitutions and laws of Latin American countries. In this chapter, we will refer to the qualities required of our legislators, so that they may conscientiously develop their lofty task.

With very few exceptions, the legislative bodies of Mexico have been composed of individuals who represent the inhabitants of their respective political entities in a theoretical or nominal manner. Mexico City and the other political centers of the federation were the fertile wombs from which the highest percentage of political representatives sprang. Many regions of the country were never represented by individuals born in them or who were even familiar with the living conditions there. This naturally contributed to the political preeminence of some regions and the marginalization of others. Because of this, we say that representation was theoretical at best.

This was especially the case during the Porfirian era. Back then, all knew that their legislators lacked a purpose, that their role was reduced to that of sleepwalking lackeys who presided over imbecilic and narcotic congressional sessions. The laws that have reigned in independent Mexico do not deserve to be called such; they are sociologically unilateral and geographically localist dispositions. Their application did not bring about the harmonious development of all of our social groups or the progress of all of the political entities of the federation. This disequilibrium is one of the causes of our current and previous revolutions. The revolution of ideas that is now taking place, a movement that is complementary to the revolution of arms, should not tend toward the reestablishment of that old social disequilibrium. Rather, it should begin to lay the foundations upon which to gradually build an equilibrated and strong national society. This can be achieved when one can rely on truly democratic legislation. To build such legislation, we must first have recourse to democratic legislators. Let us see some of the conditions that lend democratic legitimacy to legislators who can satisfactorily carry out their mandate.

A. ETHNIC REPRESENTATION

To legitimately represent the diverse ethnic groups of our population, our legislators must be named by and belong to these diverse groups, or at least be intimately acquainted with their way of life. The electoral mechanisms—except for the general means of gathering and transmitting data—shall also be those that are chosen by those diverse ethnic and regional groups, even if some seem very primitive compared with others. In effect, indigenous families conserve a deeply rooted patriarchal system that regulates electoral nominations, the settlement of local conflicts, and so forth. The federation and the governments of the states have no right to place obstacles to these proceedings, so long as they are not prejudicial to the collectivity.

The houses of congress have never known the conditions and the necessities of the Mayas of Yucatán, Quintana Roo, Campeche, Tabasco, and Chiapas; of the Otomís of Mexico, Guanajuato, and Querétaro; of the Yaquis of Sonora; of the "pintos" of Guerrero; of any of the millions of beings that make up our indigenous families. This lack of knowledge is understandable if one thinks of how few indigenous individuals have ever served in the legislature, and that those few have been individuals who abandoned their indigenous heritage. Through their own will or through the exigencies of their environment, they had assimilated the culture, the language, the aspirations, and the tendencies of other social classes. Like the legislators of white race, they did not comprehend or "see" the urgent physical and intellectual needs of their former brothers, whom they now considered to be unredeemed and uncultured. Indigenous families were separated from the national whole, ignored by the constitution and by the federal and provincial laws. They only figured in the thoughts of the dominant classes when it was time to impose arbitrary taxes on them or to deceive them through commercial transactions. This desperate situation left them with a simple choice: rebel or die. Some of these indigenous families, as can be observed in the central mesa, have been perishing through degeneracy. Others—Yaquis and Mayas—lived in eternal rebellion. Almost all of these latter groups have collaborated in the current revolution in search of their liberties.

B. DEMOGRAPHIC REPRESENTATION

The chambers should not be filled with unconscious members of the bourgeoisie, as has often been the case in Mexico. It is indispensable that all of our social groups be represented. The workers of the cities, the toilers of the fields, bureaucrats, industrialists, agriculturalists, capitalists, people of the sea, railroad workers, and so forth should possess an effective voice and vote in matters of legislation. Otherwise, laws will continue to be as they have been until today, unilateral and inadequate for the good governance of all of the social groups that constitute the nation.

C. THE REPRESENTATION OF INTELLECTUALS

In our country, men of science, cultured and independent journalists, and artists of merit have generally been distanced from politics. This is a fatal prejudice. The legislature has always been ruled by the colorless, by the mediocre. The few intellectuals who were admitted into the legislature were expected to watch, listen, and be silent, whilst the cretinous majority yawned or debated the innocuous topics imposed "from above." How can we conceive of a legislative chamber that works without the intellectual elements that in all other parts of the world have been the base and summit of national progress?

D. THE REPRESENTATION OF POLITICAL PARTIES

We have, on purpose, left political parties last. Politics! Have we ever sensibly known what that term means or what it means in our national context? One thing must be said without mincing words: Mexican politics was a heterogeneous and indistinct blend of personalisms—rife with adulation, fears, and ambitions—that enriched certain individuals and castes. A true hydra! It would be better that "politicians" play no role in our legislature, if these are to be politicians cast in the molds of yesterday.

18

Politics and Its Values

The success of any enterprise, the efficiency of any work, requires that it be composed of basic elements that have real value. In order for the collaboration of political parties in the recently reconstructed government to be useful and efficient, it is necessary for those parties to possess a practical, positive value. If our older notions of politics are to persist, it is better that political parties not reemerge.

A. THE POLITICS OF THE PAST

In general, our professional politicians have been of little value in and of themselves. They have lacked individual efficiency. Their true character becomes evident in exile, where all of those who were able to misappropriate power and money now live. Other politicians, the majority, carry on miserably, intellectually incapacitated and impotent for physical effort. In all countries, the sun shines and there is work for those who love to work. How else, but as parasites and frauds, can we refer to individuals that seem like glorious figures at home and then go to other lands to feast on embezzled monies or who would never lower themselves to earn their bread honorably? What national transcendence can we expect from associations or parties formed by this type of abnormal being?

It is sensible to say that Mexican politicians have had two convergent and clearly perceptible goals: to attain power and to attain riches. The means to reach these ends consisted primarily of adulation, an illness that fatally contaminated even those circles that were not, strictly speaking, political. Those time-tested means of gaining and maintaining power were enforced, when necessary, with threats, extortions, and bribes.

When one was wealthy, money served to do politics and reach power; political power was simply a pretension that developed naturally out of the possession of money. Of course, the power that most politicians could attain was trifling, as real power was concentrated in very few hands. Politics was, in the end, a self-perpetuating farce.

When one was poor, one did politics to scale in power, and then used this power to accumulate money through concessions, privileges, and so forth. A small minority of the truly adept, our old "political personalities," triumphed by obtaining both power and wealth. As a stepping-stone, they used the great mass of little politicians, sad men who accumulated no more power than that which was given to them by political patrons, the miserable alms that were conceded to them in recompense for imagined services and businesses. And, of course, politicians maintained this farce with the public budget, never with their own funds.

Political personalities boasted about their own virtues, spouting affected speeches that were void of any content, funding press campaigns that were full of servile adulation and crass insult but that did not contain a single idea. They threw banquets at all hours, they voluntarily sacrificed official and personal honor, they renounced human dignity in ridiculous rabble-rousing and pseudo-political rallies. These things constituted the mechanism, the way of doing politics. The little politicians, unfortunates by nature, were birthed by the work and grace of more or less influential patrons. In return for these favors, the patrons expected lifelong canine fidelity from their illegitimate political offspring. In short, this way of doing politics meant that the political lives of 15 million souls were dedicated to preserving the wealth and power of a group of political octopuses that paralyzed our national development.

This political field, which had been an obstacle to our well-being, was healed by the revolution. Today, factions that conduct this kind of politics no longer exist. And if they do exist, it is in a larval state and hidden in the muck, where they will soon die from lack of oxygen. It is also possible that some elements that appear to be revolutionary are the virulent seeds of the politics of yesteryear. In these cases, their quick extirpation is necessary.

B. THE POLITICS OF THE FUTURE

1. *The Interests*. Naïve idealists deplore the fact that politics is fundamentally a fight between different and often opposed interests. Yes, politics is a fight between interests, and cannot be anything else, as the life of peoples is conaturalized through material or abstract interests. And since every group has the right to pursue a better life, this naturally generates struggles. Why, then, is it seen as objectionable that the politics of yesteryear was representative of certain large interests? Precisely because that politics protected the interests of an insignificant minority of classes and individuals, while doing harm to the smaller interests of the vast majority of the population. This situation brought with it an immediate disequilibrium and the collapse of so unstable a base.

If, for example, all Mexicans had been *científicos*[1] during the era of Díaz, the politics that was adapted in that age would have been ideal. It would have been convenient to the well-being of all, promoting their interests equally. The tendency and end of politics should be to establish a government that seeks to promote the development and the harmonious, equal, and effective improvement of the interests of diverse social groups. A truly democratic politics is that which offers the best guarantees to the nation, given that it favors all of its interests equally.

2. *The Legitimate Origin of Politics*. Politics is born from two theoretically antagonistic entities. First, the government is established to seek the greatest well-being possible for the population and to make its presence felt in such a way that the population will continue to give it trust and support. It should also correct the deficiencies that both friends and enemies find in its administration. Second, there is oppositional politics. The term "opposition" does not necessarily mean hostility toward the government but simply opposition in certain aspirations or sensibilities. This politics should consist in studying the nature and necessities of the population from a different point of view in order to better understand the means of seeking its improvement. Possessing such data, the opposition can justifiably point out the deficiencies of the established government, as well as the advantages that a new political platform or program can provide in the future. By these means, the most competent and apt opposition party gathers popular momentum.

3. *The Personalities of Politicians*. The sudden appearance of individuals without any personal value who are considered "political personalities" should be considered ridiculous. It is no longer necessary, as it was before, to weave

---

[1] This was a common term for the technocratic political elite of the Porfiriato, referring to their identity with positivism and "scientific" governance.—Trans.

together shining little phrases or to write empty words, or to hold banquets in order to do politics. Every man that defends the rights of social groups and attacks abuses—whether he does so with eloquence or in a pedestrian way—is a politician. Beyond the doors of the legislative chambers, one finds the worker politician, the merchant politician, the capitalist politician, the agriculturalist politician, the intellectual politician. In the end, these are personalities that truly represent defined interests, be these material or abstract. Let us no longer tolerate "politician politicians," men who represent nothing and no one, but who only intrigue, exploit, and discredit the nation. It is also indispensable to sweep away the public employees who, in order to avail themselves of political power, employ the moral force and material resources of the posts that they occupy.

The most deeply rooted vice of the Mexican politician is personalism. Politicians should fight for the well-being of the groups to which they belong and the interests that these represent. They should naturally obtain the benefits that correspond to them as integral members of these groups. Before, politicians managed the groups that they supposedly represented at will, guiding their activities and making them contribute to their own personal improvement and not toward that of the collectivity to which they belonged. Today, our social groups should control the politicians that represent them and not the other way around.

Politics, or that which is thus known, was always a seedbed of corruption in Mexico. Before the new, true politics can emerge, it is necessary to disinfect the environment. It is necessary to demand this of future politicians: that they have a mandate that is broadly legitimated by moral sanctity, personal efficiency, and effective representation.

19

....

Our Religious Transition

When a people is subjugated, it is relatively easy for the conquerors to impose new art, new industries, new customs, and other manifestations of culture. But it is very difficult and time-consuming to make the conquered accept new religious ideas. Since its origins on the arid hill of Calvary, Christianity was imposed on paganism and Judaism at the cost of torrents of blood. The reformist sects achieved triumph after running through many thorny paths and leaving a trail of martyrs behind them. Almost all religious transitions have had some bloody Saint Bartholomew as their price. Why was the transition from indigenous paganism to Spanish Catholicism in the sixteenth century relatively easy? How is it that only Catholicism has been implanted among us, in spite of active—if pointless—attempts to introduce Protestantism?

The transition from indigenous paganism to Catholicism found no obstacles because the two religions shared certain elements that were propitious to their fusion. In contrast, paganism and Protestantism are dissimilar in essence and form. Catholicism was not imposed by the biting scourge, or by the Sacred Office, or by the charity of the missions. Had it been, rivers of blood would have flowed in Mexico as well. It is well-known that attempts at rebellion during the Colonial period were fights brought on by hunger, lack of land, oppression, and a thousand other causes, but almost never by struggles over religion.

The soul of the indigene was gently occupied by Catholicism. The old pagan myths fused with the faith of the Roman Church, were transformed by it, or died quietly. The religious ideas of the pre-Hispanic groups of Mexico differ from one another in terms of their external modalities but were similar

90

enough to make some generalizations. To prove my previous assertions about our religious transition, one can choose any of those religions, such as the Azteco-Teotihuacán, which has interesting historical antecedents and profuse representations in the archaeological record.

The indigenous deities had an abstract origin; they were fabulous and humanly inexplicable. However, their means of manifesting themselves to humans was very objective, as they are always shown in the form of persons or diverse animals and objects. Each of those gods reigned over a clearly delimited range of intellectual and material activities. Worship and ritual were symbolic, eye-catching, and complex. Thus, the Aztec god of war was symbolized by a bundle of hummingbird feathers that fell into the breast of his mother, a pious woman of Coatlán, as she was sweeping the temple. The prodigious infant had human form but wore a beautiful headdress of hummingbird feathers on his left leg and the beak of the same bird upon his face. His worship was bloody, with anthropophagic communion; dances and songs; the use of blood and burning copal, mica, and charcoal; maguey paper; and rubber. This god was the tutelary deity of war, so that good harvests, rains, and other gifts were not sought from him.

These attributions of divinity were extremely diverse. There were 400 gods of pulque (so we should not be scandalized by the number of pulquerias nowadays). Chaste and lustful love, death, maternity, and old age were each presided over or depended upon one or more deities. So did air, fire, water, the stars, the months, and all that was tangible to the senses and intelligence in the physical and psychic world. The limitless number of gods consecrated in the Valley of Mexico becomes clear in a mythological fable, probably of Teotihuacán origin, that tells of their birth. The original couple of gods, denizens of the seventeenth heaven, conceived an obsidian knife rather than a divine offspring as their last child. Disgusted, its siblings threw it to the earth, where it shattered into a thousand pieces, each of which gave birth to a flaming god.

Let us now see how Catholicism was presented to and taken up by the Aztecs. The Indian saw in the Mother of God the quintessential synthesis of feminine deities and considered her a major goddess. Jesus Christ entered the pre-Hispanic Olympus as the first of the gods. However, God the Father was not comprehensible to those iconolophiles, because of his abstract conception and lack of a material representation. The Aztecs accepted the Roman calendar with all of its saints, because these seemed few in contrast to their own gods.

The Indians adhered to the dogmas and mysteries of the new religion without comprehending them, just as the mysteries of the old pagan religion had been adhered to dogmatically. The recently arrived gods had human form and were represented like the old gods, in wooden or stone effigies painted with the same lively colors as the ritual codices. The Catholic deity, like the pagan ones, punished and rewarded, took away illnesses, saved harvests, brought rains. Finally, the pompous Roman ritual, with its gold and inlays, the shine of bronzes, the light of a thousand candles, the dense clouds of incense, and the imposing religious music, reminded the conquered of the glorious days in which priests in white tunics gravely ascended the steps of the temple, murmuring orations and shaking flags of paper spattered with drops of rubber, while the sacred braziers smoked ceaselessly above, veiling the inscrutable faces of the deities as the multitude below was moved into a great silence of fear and faith.

It was, then, logical that the indigenes of Mexico voluntarily accepted the Catholic creed and rejected a Protestantism that seemed abstract, exotic, iconoclastic, and incomprehensible to them.

20

Our Catholics

The immense majority of our population professes Catholicism, without admitting argument or doubt. Unfortunately, not all of us are *sensibly* Catholic. In Mexico, there are three types of Catholics: Pagan Catholics, True Catholics, and Utilitarian Catholics.

A. PAGAN CATHOLICS

Although they are the majority, they constitute the intellectually and socially inferior elements of the population. It would require them twenty, fifty, or more years to acquire the religion, language, and culture that are indispensable for their incorporation into civilization. We will cite a few relevant cases of this mixed religion. In the Sierra de Zongolica in the State of Veracruz, spread along the rivers Tontos, Coyolapan, and Altototonga, there are Indians of diverse ethnic affiliations: Popolocas, Mixtecs, Zapotecs. If the parish churches are not too far away, all of these Indians confirm their children, marry, and die in the bosom of the Catholic Church. Still, many other ceremonies that are of great importance in their lives show the clear seal of paganism. When their milpas are about to germinate and sprout tender shoots, they consider it indispensable that an old Indian who knows mysterious conjurations preserves the plants from voracious pests, especially the deer that come down from the mountain on moonlit nights. We have been witnesses of the curious rite and can describe it faithfully. The wise old Indian, a true priest of this race, chants in Aztec, in a tearful and supplicant tone, and begs the Deer God to calm his children, the forest deer. Later, under a great ceiba tree that filters the light of the moon, braziers burn with little sacrificed birds, horn scrapings and dear hooves, strips of paper made from wild banana leaf, and amber-colored grains of copal incense, all tossed in by the blackened hand of the Indian sorcerer. It burns in fleeting white clouds.

This is an intermediate example of Pagan Catholicism. Some of the groups that we denominate as Pagan Catholics are more inclined toward paganism, and others are more inclined toward Catholicism. Amongst the former we include primitive tribes, the Huicholes, Coras, Seris, Tepehuanes, Lacandónes, and so forth. Go to the museum, and you will see the gods, idols carved in stone, wood, and ferns, that those tribes currently "use." The latter include Indians who live close to the cities, the uncultured rabble of the city itself, and other people who are neither Indians nor part of the rabble but who commune with pagan superstition. Have we not seen the dancers that come year after year to Remedios or Tacuba to sing and dance in the parish atria, crowned with headdresses of feathers and foil just as they had worn in the teocallis of their ancestors? Do we not know how the thugs of Tepito and La Palma kneel before the Virgen de Soledad as before the warlike Huitzilopochtli, pleading for a firm grip with which to handle their knives in the next homicide? Are there not young ladies that hang Saint Anthony from his feet or naïve ranchers that put out the candle of Saint Isidro because they do not see their wishes granted?

All of this is Pagan Catholicism or Catholic Paganism, however one wishes to call it.

B. TRUE CATHOLICS

These are firm, sincere believers who are free of conventionalisms. They are conscious of their ideas and have the valor to sustain them. They are liberal regarding the ideas of others. These Catholics flog the merchants in the temple. From their lips always fall two sentences that are very convenient for our country: "Render unto Caesar what is Caesar's" and "My reign is not of this world." They understand the infinite nature of divinity with a generous sensibility. They are not complacent with having the saints to scare away spiders or mice, or with finding lost needles and rings. They take science as science and religion as religion.

True Catholics understand that fanaticism is offensive to God, and they themselves flee from fanatics as if they were the plague. The clergy that cultivates these Catholics serves as a fine moral example and exercises a noble social function in Mexico. Respect and guarantees should be extended to these True Catholics.

C. UTILITARIAN CATHOLICS

The Pagan Catholics are not culpable for their errors; they need help and piety. It is necessary to educate them religiously and civilly. The True Catholics are worthy of all esteem and respect. However, the Utilitarian Catholics deserve to be thrust from the bosom of church and nation. They are those that do politics, stalk the land, and kill when they can, all beneath the mantle of religion. Because of their fanaticism, they would reinstitute the Inquisition. Because of their avarice, they would once again sell Christ, only for more money than Judas did. Because of their cowardice, they would deny the Lord so many times that there would not be enough roosters in the world to call them out.

Utilitarian Catholics promote a politicized clergy that is a natural enemy of the True Catholics. Those individuals want to make their bastard ideas triumph through prayers and religious functions but would never take a cent from their own pockets to sustain or promote them. They leave the actual practice of religion to their wives, their daughters, and their sisters, while they watch the rosary beads pass by in a cowardly and hypocritical way. But what is most revolting and inspires the most indignation is that when one of these men sees his dirty dealings destroyed or attacked before all of the other Mexican Catholics, he hides among them. The Utilitarian Catholics set the True Catholics before themselves like a bulwark or trench to resist the first blow—or all of them if possible! Because of this, it is unlikely that the True Catholics, the respectable and worthy ones, will remain unharmed when the pernicious and utilitarian ones are persecuted. It is very unfortunate that the pastoral of the Archbishop of Quito, Ecuador, Sr. D. Federico González Suárez, published in the Mexican press some years ago and in which the bishop hurls anathemas at the Utilitarian Catholics, did not become more popular in our country.

21

Our Intellectual Culture

Our manifestations of culture have traditionally been irregular, particularly in the fine arts and the social sciences. That deficiency has two primary causes. First, there is the ethnic heterogeneity of our population, which means that there is not a truly national environment for harmonic and defined intellectual production. The second cause is the feudal intellectualism, which has always developed amongst us in a way parallel to governmental exclusivism. We will examine these two causes of our intellectual stagnation.

A. ETHNIC HETEROGENEITY

The population of Mexico is formed by three classes or groups, each of which is clearly defined by its ethnic, social, and cultural differences.

1. *The First Group*. This group is composed ethnically of individuals of indigenous race or of those in whom indigenous blood predominates. From the social or hierarchical perspective, these individuals have always been servants, pariahs, the disinherited, the oppressed. Their slavery has lasted from when Hernán Cortés placed the iron bridle of Spain upon them until 1910, when the revolution told the Indian to abandon his lethargy.

But even if the deepest roots of the revolution germinated and continue to germinate with the indigenous race, it was not begun by them. This seems paradoxical, if we consider that the indigenous population is the most numerous, possesses the greatest physical energies, and has experienced the worst slavery.

96

The explanation for this contradiction is very clear. The Indian, destined to suffer, was always disposed to avenge abuses, thefts, and oppression, even at the cost of his own life. But unfortunately, he did not know the appropriate means with which to attain his own liberation. He lacks directive abilities, which are only obtained through the possession of scientific knowledge and the convenient orientation of certain manifestations of culture. In effect, the indigenous uprisings that took place during the Colonial period generally failed because of a lack of direction. The revolution for independence was fought at the expense of Indian blood but was conceived and developed by brains that were not Indian. The reform was achieved in an identical manner, as Benito Juarez and others like him are exceptions that prove this rule of the lack of direction that is typical of the Indian.

This situation has been particularly clear in the Revolution of 1910. Two social classes, two races were the primary contributors to its victory. In the north, elements of mixed race dominated (the intermediate race that we will refer to later). In the south, the Indian race was the rebel majority. Both groups shared the same valor, energy, and just aspirations. Nonetheless, it was the north that began and developed the revolution and consummated its triumph, even if those in the south shed so much more blood.

Why is it that the Indian does not know how to conceive, direct, and lead to victory his revolutions when he constitutes the majority of the population, possibly has superior physical energies, and has intellectual aptitudes comparable to those of any race in the world? This is because of the mode of being, the evolutionary state of our indigenous civilization, the intellectual state in which these individuals find themselves. Let us examine the culture and intellectual heritage of the indigenous race with an ethnological sensibility.

If we examine the religious beliefs, artistic tendencies, industrial activities, domestic customs, and ethical modalities of the Indian, we can see that he lives in a backwardness of 400 years, even if he conserves vigorous mental aptitudes. His intellectual achievements are a continuation of those that developed in pre-Hispanic times, only reformed by the circumstances of his environment. Naturally, however brilliant and surprisingly developed pre-Hispanic civilization was for its time, the traces of it that we see today seem anachronistic, inappropriate, and impractical. There are indigenes who have a surprising knowledge of the course of the sun, the moon, and other celestial bodies. In pre-Columbian times, these individuals would have been respected astrologer-priests. But now, they would seem ridiculous if they were installed in an astronomical observatory. Indian herbalists that possess the secret of a vast medicinal pharmacopeia would have justly been considered medical notables in the past, but our modern doctor disdains them and accuses them of being untrained poisoners. The very interesting Indian storytellers who relate the adventures of the coyote, the serpent, the nagual,[1] the moon, the sun, the forests, and the lakes could once have been the signature literatos of the Aztec court, although today not even the folklorist gives them all of the attention that they deserve.

There is, nevertheless, one thing in which this knowledge with roots in the pre-Hispanic past was superior to contemporary knowledge. We refer to psychic phenomena: magnetism, suggestion, telepathy, and so forth. The Indian "sorcerers"[2] are well-known, individuals worthy of study by our ethnologists and psychologists. Sorcerers can—or so they say—summon spirits. They do this with the spirits of murder victims, which they make confront their murderers, thus making it easy to find the culprit. The sorcerer turns the scornful into lovers and can cause misfortune, illness, misery, and even death to his enemies by performing all of the offenses that he wishes upon him on a mannequin. The complicated ceremonies of the sorcerer bring about a series of actions and reactions on unknown energies. This is nothing less than what occurs with magnetism, hypnotism, and telepathy. The scholars of today, contemporary sorcerers, approach these phenomena with the same vague knowledge as the Indian sorcerers, who would have been the sages of the pre-Hispanic age.

The Indian continues to cultivate a more or less reformed pre-Hispanic culture and will continue to do so until he is gradually, logically, and sensibly incorporated into contemporary civilization. In the past, this incorporation has been attempted by indoctrinating him with religious ideas or by simply dressing him up in city clothes and teaching him the alphabet, as if he were a member of one of our other classes. Naturally, that civilizing bath has not penetrated further than the epidermis; the Indian's body and soul remain as pre-Hispanic as ever. We do not intend to incorporate the Indian by "Europeanizing" him in a single blow. On the contrary, we should "Indianize" ourselves a bit, offer our civilization to him in a form that is diluted with his own. Then, he will not find this civilization exotic, cruel, bitter, and incomprehensible. But naturally, our approximation to the Indian should not be exaggerated to a ridiculous extreme.

We can conclude that the Indian possesses his own civilization, which, as attractive as it might be and as high an evolutionary grade as it represents, is backward in relation to contemporary civilization. Modern civilization, being

---

[1] "Nagual" is the Nahuatl term used for a broader set of animal spirits or shape-changing sorcerers in several indigenous societies.—Trans.

[2] Sp. *Brujos*.—Trans.

partly of scientific character, leads to better practical results and contributes to our material and intellectual well-being with greater efficacy.

2. *The Second Group.* The second group of the population to which we have referred is composed of individuals of mixed blood, including those in which the proportion of European, and especially Spanish, blood predominates. In ethnic terms, this group has always been the source of our *mestizaje*. Socially, this class has been an eternal rebel, an enemy of the class of pure foreign blood, and the author and director of riots and revolutions. This class has understood the just laments of the indigenous class and taken advantage of its latent energies. It has always used these energies as a lever to contain the operations of power. Concerning the intellectual culture of this "middle class," we can say without exaggeration that it is the only class that produces or that has produced intellectually in our country.

Unfortunately, the intellectual production of this class is marked by a series of tendencies that could not be considered properly nationalist. Since the Colonial period, the Spanish tended to impose European and especially Spanish intellectual sensibilities. Besides the fact that it represents a more advanced evolutionary grade, European culture was diffused more methodically. In contrast, indigenous culture was not systematized; it did not form a school. It was kept and cultivated by the masses without special promoters and propagates itself spontaneously.

The intermediate group of our society then found itself in a terrible disjuncture. On one hand, it felt the enormous weight of the cultural sensibilities of the indigenous class. On the other, the exotic sensibility imported and imposed by the Spanish dominators also influenced the middle class. From this situation was born what we could call a cultural schism. A large part of the middle class felt more at home in the physical environment in which it developed and with the historical antecedents that brought it close to the indigenous class. It adopted an intermediate culture that was neither Indian nor occidental. This preference is justified if one considers that the topography of the land, the bases of nutrition, the animal population, and the historical antecedents of Mexico are different from those of the old continent. The physico-biological-social environment, which is always the origin of a people's intellectual and material manifestations, impelled the intermediate class to adopt the sensibilities of the indigenous class and reject those of the European.

We will cite some examples of this culture. The music of the people, which Ponce is making known with such notable efforts, is neither Indian nor

European. Its technique and mechanical dimension are occidental, but its character strongly evokes the Indian soul. Sculptors from Mexico and Guadalajara who make statuettes of clay or wax and traditionally decorated vases are the true national sculptors, however foolishly the public considers their works to be mere knick-knacks. The decorations used in the lacquer industry, in tile, clothing, and a thousand other things, are the true Mexican decorations. They were inspired by our sky, our soil, our flowers, our animals, and even the ancient polytheistic religious concepts of the pre-Hispanic Indians. More could be said about literature, architecture, and the very special form that religious ideas take among this intermediate class.

This intermediate culture, like that of the indigenous class, developed without scientific principles, methods, and facilities. It has some obvious deficiencies and deformations, like anything that flowered after overcoming obstacles. Nevertheless, this is the national culture, the culture of our destiny, which will finish imposing itself when the population is ethnically homogeneous enough to feel and comprehend it. Whoever knows about the origins, evolution, and state of Japanese culture will understand why we are justified in talking about our intermediate culture in this way.

From the sociological perspective, it is important to examine the minority of this intermediate group that we refer to as "schismatic." They are those who rejected indigenous culture in its entirety and embraced the occidental. Schismatic painters copy Murillo, Rubens, Zuloaga. Or what is worse, they paint things pertinent to France, Spain, Italy, and even China, but never Mexico. Schismatic sculptors sculpt the Greek Olympus and disdain the Mexican. It is clear that when this art is exhibited, the majority of Mexicans who view it are left feeling empty. They do not contemplate something of their own or that is in their life, environment, and soul.

There is a type of art that is even more reproachable. Persons identified with European aesthetic sensibilities try to produce artwork that incorporates indigenous or pre-Hispanic motifs and elements, without knowing the spirit that originated these or without knowing about their historical or artistic antecedents. What results is a hybrid artwork, born of European ideas but presented in American forms.

Amongst the "schismatics" we also count notable sociologists and psychologists. But what deception! These gentlemen have read as much Spencer and James as arrives to us in the latest steamship; know all about the social problems of Germany, France, and even Turkestan; and even about the psychology of New Zealanders. But they know nothing, or seem to know nothing, about our sociology or our psychology. With very few exceptions, nothing is researched or published about our environment. When the sociologist or psychologist attempts a study of our own population, prejudices are evident in his every step. If he deduces laws and expounds on theories, these are applicable for every country but ours. This is a logical result of the fact that our sociologists have never descended from their lofty peaks to touch the people and sense their soul. They only contemplate the population from afar in their offices and through foreign authors whose writings they draw on and accept dogmatically.

In the right time and place, one can accept the means, methods, and "how to's" of European civilization. But we do not want our social substance to have the same molecules and properties as the European. We do not pretend that both cultures can be emptied into the same mold or that they can be directed to the same ends. This "schismatic culture" is not and will never be our national culture. Nor is it truly occidental. In order to possess a given culture, it is indispensable to live in an environment where this culture originated and developed. "Schismatic culture" is the patrimony of pedants and imbeciles.

3. *The Third Group*. This part of our population is constituted ethnically by individuals who are the near or distant descendants of foreigners established in our country, whose blood has mixed very little with the middle class and not at all with the indigenes. Socially, they make up the aristocracy. When rich, these individuals form a medieval Masonic organization. When they are poor, it is sad to say that they are an embarrassing and useless mass.

Can there be a true intellectual production in a country in which cultural tendencies are this anachronistic, heterogeneous, and divergent? We think not.

B. FEUDAL INTELLECTUALISM

Having examined the obstacles to our intellectual culture imposed by ethnic heterogeneity, let us examine them from another point of view. One often criticizes the *cacicazgo*[3] of rulers, landowners, and capitalists, but intellectual *cacicazgos* are never mentioned or castigated. Nevertheless, this national plague is well-known. It only takes for an individual—legitimately or fraudulently—to

----

[3] *Cacicazgo* is Spanish for "chiefdom." Although this word originally referred to indigenous communities, it is expanded in Mexican vernacular Spanish to refer to any patron-client, personalist, or extra-official power bloc.—Trans.

acquire the image of intellectual for him to adopt two prerogatives. The first consists in maintaining himself at the grade or stage of intellectualism in which he was met by public recognition, be this true recognition or the product of his self-promotion. Thus consecrated, he will never study again, will not admit new ideas or orientations, will detest the continuous advancement of science. He will only pontificate. Such an error is not, in and of itself, of great transcendence, for in the end, it is the decision of every individual whether he continues to study or hides his head under his wing like an ostrich. What is inexcusable is that the consecrated one—whether because of his real merits or through charlatanism—takes it upon himself to contain, suffocate, and annihilate all others who dare to enter into "his" field. That is, by touching upon a field of study, he monopolizes it.

In the good times of General Díaz, there were two or three consecrated "courtly" historians. The same could be said of sociologists, psychologists, archaeologists, painters, and so forth. The young men who brought with them new ideas, those who had touched upon the new purified truth, were rejected. The court intellectuals tried to disorient them, discourage them. If they persisted, they were condemned to intellectual ostracism. The doors that would have allowed them entry into the field of ideas were closed, and many lost the means of earning their livelihood.

When General Díaz fell, many of those sackcloth pontiffs tumbled down with him, and many continue to fall. Now that we see them, grotesquely unmasked, it is amazing that they held such intellectual tyranny for so long. Ethnic heterogeneity will persist for a long time as an obstacle to our intellectual production. On the other hand, feudal intellectualism and the *cacicazgo* of ideas are disappearing and should disappear completely.

22

The Concept of Culture

Culture . . . civilization . . . progress. . . . What absolute or even relative value can one attribute to these terms? Overcoming the inevitable sensation of sloth that comes with the anticipation of muscular exertion, we went to leaf through the several pounds of paper with which the Royal Academy fixes and gives splendor to the language of Cervantes. But in the end, we changed our mind, and the respectable hulk remained untouched and serene on its cedar shelf. Such a consultation would have given us an academic definition of these terms, or a Spanish one, or one pertinent to all of Europe. But since our culture is not academic, or Spanish, or European, such a definition would have been exotic to our sensibilities. What's more, the current European war has "modernized" the concept of culture, giving it a flexibility that makes it bounce like a rubber ball.

Any Mexican who has been in Europe or North America has undoubtedly seen that we are graced with the label of "an uncultured people" by the uninformed, by pedants, and even by men who aspire to illustration. The statement is not something to cry over, but it does move one to dot all his i's.

Modern anthropology has established the fact that culture is the conjunction of all of the material and intellectual features that characterize human groups. It does not attempt to establish grades regarding cultural superiority or to anachronistically characterize peoples as cultured or uncultured. Culture is developed by the collective minds of peoples; it emerges from their historical antecedents and from the environment and circumstances that surround them. That is to say, each people has the culture that is inherent to its ethnico-social nature and the physical and biological conditions of the ground that they inhabit. It is not sensible for any people to think of its *cultura* or *Kultur* or culture as superior to those of others, or try to impose it by force. When people have tried to do this, they have only succeeded in creating a new culture, the product of a fusion between the invaded and invasive culture. Or, in other cases, the invaded culture persists and the invasive culture disintegrates under the influence of its new environment.

Mexico offers a typical example of this phenomenon. European culture has been fighting uselessly for various centuries in order to establish itself among us. Nevertheless, that culture only exists with an artificial life and among small social groups. The social groups that we have referred to as "intermediate," which are far more numerous in this country, possess industry, dress, literature, plastic and graphic arts, music, religious and moral concepts, traditions, and other manifestations of a culture that is not European. In short, all that constitutes our typical culture is distinct from both European and indigenous cultural types, despite being derived from them. Besides this "intermediate" group, the indigenous families that represent much more than half of our population possess an autochthonous culture, since they have not been able to or have not wanted to assimilate much of the invading culture.

Furthermore, we should ask if it is true that the most cultured people is the one that possesses the greatest sense of morality, the best aesthetic judgment, the most ample scientific knowledge, the highest intellectuality—overall, the greatest wealth and power. One would have to admit that a people that unified such superior gifts harmoniously in their own lives would be the most cultured. But where are they? This people has never existed, not in Classic Rome, not in heroic Greece, not in the time of the pharaohs, not in the nebulosity of the Quaternary period. If we were to find such an objective example as a basis for our speculation, we must let the futurist thinkers go and seek it in other worlds. In effect, no people has ever unified all of the physical and intellectual characteristics that represent the highest degree of evolution. It seems as if a law of compensation or equilibrium prevents one people from reaching integral perfection over another. We can cite several examples: the pronounced development of the wealth of a people generally comes with a marked artistic flowering and a decadence or relaxation of the moral order (as in Egypt and Rome). Likewise, the experience of history shows us that a truly democratic form of governance tends to favor the development of ethical ideas and weakens or paralyzes aesthetic ideas (as in the North American republic in its earliest times). In general, we should note that the characteristics of a culture are not produced in accordance with fixed principles, but arbitrarily. Therefore, it is not possible to establish authorized quantitative comparisons between peoples. For example, art is not formed through determined rules, but naturally. It is illogical to say that the art of one people is superior to another's or vice versa, since there are no bases to establish relativity. The same happens with religion, philosophy, customs, and so forth.

As we said, the term "culture" means the sum of material and intellectual characteristics that distinguish and differentiate human groups amongst themselves, but "culture" never connotes the quality of these manifestations. Perhaps the ideas presented here will offend traditionalists, and they will blame us for not recognizing the integral progress of humanity. In that case, they would be right, since we frankly do not believe in such progress. Human morality never advanced ascendantly. It has its highs and lows. In all men, from the semi-zoological ones of 100,000 years ago until the contemporary ones, the sentiments of individual and social egoism have reigned above all others. Abstract or material possessions constitute the key, the explanation for all impulses. Before, one crushed the skull of an enemy to throw him out of his cave and take it over. Today, one poisons him with gas, the product of marvelous chemistry, to rip territory and commerce from him. It is only a matter of method.

The same repetition and continuity can be seen in the more valuable creations of human groups. The interesting and abstract monotheism that the pharaoh Akhenaton conceived thousands of years before Christ does not cede anything in idealism or beauty to the most purified of our current theosophist concepts. Who can affirm that polytheistic ideas and other creeds will not reappear among us, as happened after the monotheistic period of the aforementioned pharaoh? Art flowers, decays, and resurges, and some of our more "evolved" aesthetic sensibilities have precedents in other times and among other peoples. Rodinesque expressionism can be found in the little Teotihuacán heads from more than twelve centuries ago and in the Aztec sculptures of Tenochtitlán.[1] The abstract forms that have gained such fame because of the so-called modernist decoration could be substituted and improved by the profuse and original Maya stylization.

The same can be said regarding customs. Saluting with the hat or the hand, dressing in mourning, wearing medals and badges, and so forth are persistences or reappearances of conventionalisms as old as humanity. One cannot, then, speak of integral and ascendant progress of human manifestations of culture.

---

[1] In the original, this instance is given the nonstandard spelling Tenoxtitlán.—Trans.

There is only temporal and periodic progress, which is inevitably followed by decadence and disintegration.

We will cite an exception that proves the rule. Perhaps we can believe in progress in science, in spite of the sophistic affirmations of "nihil sub sole novum." No one has been able to demonstrate the previous historical existence of the newest conclusions of physics, chemistry, mechanics, or cosmography. Icarus, the philosopher's stone, the Egyptian crane, and the Tonalamatl or Aztec ritual calendar are the lower steps that have led man in the ascendant march toward the airplane, material transmutation, the automobile, and the orbits of the stars. But the possession of scientific knowledge does not connote superiority or inferiority in the culture of peoples, since the individuals who possess it come from a specialized caste within the population to which they belong and are distanced mentally from the other classes. The scientists of all countries form amongst themselves a universal fraternity based on the communion of their ideas.

In summary, we propose that peoples not be labeled cultured or uncultured, since this is equivalent to qualifying them as human or inhuman, corporeal or incorporeal, since culture connotes a series of manifestations inherent to human nature. Respiration, nutrition, reproduction, and so forth are physiological phenomena or manifestations of human nature. Perception, sensation, memory are its psychological manifestations. Yet it does not occur to anyone to say that Mexicans are psychologically or physiologically inferior to other peoples, much less that they lack physiology or psychology. Is it not just as naïve to say that we are uncultured or lacking in culture?

We would accept the statements that the percentage of Mexicans who possess scientific knowledge is very reduced; the percentage of individuals who do not know how to read is very high; art of European origin is not understood by the majority of the population; the products of industry are quite reduced; and so forth. We would respond that scientific knowledge is deficient in Mexico, because the character of the evolution that we have experienced for centuries makes any other way of being impossible. At present, a scientific flowering in Mexico would be extraordinary, and it is pointless to speak of extraordinary things. A majority of Mexicans do not know how to read, but they know how to do other things: they produce literary works, music, and so forth. That is to say, they lack one cultural manifestation, literacy, but possess others. Mexican industry is inferior to European, which can be explained by the richness of the soil and the ease of subsistence. It is true that we do not comprehend, we do not "feel," European art. But nor do the Europeans comprehend or feel our art.

In the final analysis, let us live happily with the natural evolution of our own culture and take those aspects of European culture that our necessities would counsel us to incorporate. We implore the Foreign Cultural God to give us the grace of His redemptive zeal and to continue to impose His culture on Asia and Africa by the force of cannons, flasks of whiskey, and missionaries. Or that He may say His last word in Europe through the battle for the superiority of one "culture" over another.

23

Language and Our Country

Some time ago, the feasibility and convenience of purifying and standardizing the ways that we speak and write the Spanish language were discussed at great length. The attempt was laudable in that it embodied a cultural goal but was illogical and impossible. Here, we will not occupy ourselves with the numerous indigenous languages and dialects that are spoken in Mexico. Rather, we will contend with the diversity of our Spanishes. Our Spanish is the Spanish of Yucatán, which is a Maya-Spanish; the Spanish of the high plateaus, which is influenced by Aztec and Otomí; that of Sonora, which is mixed with the speech of the Yaquis; that of Oaxaca, which is mixed with Zapotec; and so on and so on. We must account for the fact that our Spanish is also the Anglicized Spanish of the border region, with its particular sounds, and the Spanish of Veracruz with its own sounds, and so forth.

All of these modalities of Castilian differ from one another in terms of analogy, syntax, phonetics, and the ideology that they encapsulate. Expressions and sounds used in different regions differ insofar as Mexicans have not yet melded into a physically and intellectually homogeneous race. For this fusion to occur, it is important for a race to live in a region where physical and biological conditions are equal for all of the individuals that constitute it. The form and structure of the human body and the characteristics of its intellect—art, language, and so forth—result directly from the influences of the food, climate, flora, fauna, and geology of the land that it inhabits. The distinct regions that constitute our country vary climatologically, botanically, zoologically, and geologically. Because of this, the same Spanish will never be spoken in all of

Mexico, but we will speak the varieties that develop and flower naturally in each region.

Four hundred years of experience are more conclusive than the ideas of all the literatos and grammarians regarding the attempted unification of the Spanish language. For example, let us consider the experience of the population of white race in Yucatán, direct descendants of the Spaniards who spoke Castilian Spanish when they emigrated there in the sixteenth century. These people have a series of physiological and anatomical characteristics that were imprinted upon them by the environment. Especially notable are the pale complexion caused by tropical anemia and the form of the cranium. It would not be difficult to prove scientifically that these transformations are products of the environment, just as Dr. Boas demonstrated very perceptible cranial differences in the first generation of Hebrew immigrants to New York.

Regarding the Spanish that the Yucatecos speak, it is easily demonstrated that it differs by various degrees from that spoken in other regions of Mexico, and even more from that of the Iberian Peninsula. Their phoneticism includes obscure vowels, consonants produced by the soft palate, consonants interrupted by the closing of the glottis, and other sounds that do not exist in the Spanish that we speak in Mexico City or that is spoken by the people of Madrid. The usual vocabulary contains numerous "Mayismos." The syntax of the sentence is often altered by indigenous word concepts. Something similar happens in other regions of the country. And if this occurs in the population of Spanish descent, it is even more accentuated in the mixed and aboriginal population that has had more time living in the locality.

That literature is written among us in the Spanish of Castile, and that its authors read it with impeccable prosody for academic ears, is both possible and praiseworthy. But we should also insist that no barriers be placed on regional literature or on the cultivation of Spanish as it is naturally spoken and written in each region of the country. There is more beauty, more realism, and greater expressive power in that picturesque variety of "Spanishes" in Mexico than in any grotesque imitation of the Spanish of Castile into which they could be forcibly melded.

24

National Literature

These lines do not pretend to be didactic or to conceal an attempt at erudite criticism. They are a superficial attempt to present general observations about our national literature. That fatal xenophilic orientation that has prevailed in Mexico, our servile fidelity to foreign academic opinions, that whole false gospel to which we offer worship rather than to truth and common sense, has caused our general concept of national literature to suffer from great deficiencies.

The Royal Academy says that literature is "the genre of productions of human understanding that has as its immediate or remote goal to *express the beautiful* through the word. *Grammar, rhetoric, and poetry of all classes; the novel; eloquence; and history* are considered to be encompassed by this genre." In this sense, he who writes for subjects not mentioned by that institution—geography, archaeology, ethnology, and so forth—does not produce literary work. But even if the Royal Academy's definition of literature is not entirely satisfactory, the one that reigns among us is even less so. We circumscribe literature around poetry and the novel, excluding the work of history. As a result, we never think of the chroniclers of the Conquest, whose prose contains great beauty, as literatos, whereas we admit many authors of detestable prose and poetry into Parnassus. The error here consists in thinking that that which is beautiful is beautiful as long as it agrees with the sensibilities of a select few, and as long as it is cut to this pattern as if it were a length of cloth.

In our humble opinion, literature is what is written about any subject matter without exception, as each of these subjects can demonstrate certain kinds of beauty. What makes literature beautiful depends on the nature of men and peoples, and the environment in which they develop. Having established this, let us now take on the theme of national literature. What books, what authors are typical representations of our national literature?

The majority of those who read think that nearly all that was written during the Colonial period were dry chronicles and tiresome theological tracts. Regarding the independence period, they think that all pens were dedicated to the glorification or vilification of the independence movement. They suppose, in short, that the literary production of that period was poor and the historical production rich. They think, in turn, that literature reached great heights between the second half of the last century and today. This is an erroneous judgment, based on the simple fact that the production of what is baselessly called *belle literature* has become more profuse in recent times.

Breaking with these prejudices, we would argue that more beauty is to be found in what was written during the Colonial period and during independence than in contemporary writings. This could be because the older authors offered more veracity, more realism, than recent ones. It might be said that the literary work of contemporary authors is more pure, more elegant, more advanced than that of the others. But this is simply a natural outcome of the evolution of form. That is to say, the fact that the form of recent literature is beautiful does not preclude the fact that older forms were beautiful in their own age. The essential beauty of a literary work does not age or decay; it does not evolve. It is the same; it is the eternal and immutable beauty of yesterday, today, and tomorrow.

What is, according to the masses, the best national literature from our current period? Those who are closest to the truth say that it is to be found in writers like Angel de Campo, Payno, Fernández Lizardi,[1] Facundo, and others. Those authors are representative of what we have referred to as the intermediate classes that make up the majority of the readers within the population. Nevertheless, the number of readers of this class is very small in proportion to our overall population, since the great mass of the social elements that form the base of our nationality are excluded from this group. Given this situation, there are those who would grant a genuine nationalist quality to the singers of the rabble, among whom the Vanegas Arroyos and the Juan Panaderos[2] stand

----

[1] Angel de Campo y Valle (1868–1908), Manuel Payno, (1810–1894), José Joaquín Fernández de Lizardi (d. 1827).—Trans.

[2] Antonio Vanegas Arroyo (1852–1917); Juan Panadero is a common character in vernacular music traditions.—Trans.

out. This is, however, not necessarily the case. We must take into account that, although the people of the middle classes are numerically fewer than those of the lower classes, the number of people who read is much lower in the lower classes than in the middle. Quantitatively, the Vanegas Arroyos and Juan Panaderos are more nationalist, since they represent a greater majority of the population. But the group represented by Angel de Campo, Payno, Fernández Lizardi, and Facundo is *qualitatively* more nationalist. Although they represent a smaller quantity of the population, this minority is more literarily conscious.

For the readers who take delight in reading through foreign literary sources, principally the Spanish and French ones, the best national literature is that represented by the Gutierrez Najeras, the Tabladas, the Rebolledos, the Nervos.[3] We think that work of this genre is very beautiful but that it presents a strong, deeply rooted exotic essence and therefore lacks a truly nationalist character. Other authors with very interesting tendencies are emerging. Their work appears to be in part from the middle classes and in part from the lower classes. One can see the great transcendence of the task that they have barely initiated.

Indianists who are prone to exaggeration naïvely affirm that the only form of literary production that displays a legitimately national character is that which flowered before the Conquest. They authorize their opinion by citing beautiful works of Maya or Aztec literature. We think that this opinion is erroneous. Not being a currently productive genre, pre-Hispanic literature cannot be national in character, however much it might have been in its age. Yet, we are the first to recognize its undeniable beauty and consider it to be one of the fundamental historical bases upon which our national literature is formed. Since a few of our readers are perhaps not familiar with that literature, we suggest that they read the poems of Netzahualcoyotl, which are reproduced in various historical works. In what follows, we copy a passage from the famous "Sacred Book of the Quiches"[4] relating the creation of the universe.

> [A]ll was suspended, all calm and silent, all immobile and still; the immense expanse of the skies was deserted. And in the heart of the darkness the world was created, because the nature and the life of humanity make up the heart of he who is the heart of the sky and whose name is Huracán . . . the Creator and the Former, the Father and the Mother of life . . . he for whom

---

[3] Amado Nervo (1870–1919), Manuel Gutierrez Najera (1859–1895), José Juán Tablada (1870–1945), and Efrén Rebolledo (1877–1929).—Trans.

[4] This refers to the text now commonly known as the Popol Vuj.—Trans.

all moves and breathes, father and enlivener of the peace of people and their
civilized centers. He whose wisdom has meditated over the excellence of
all that exists in the sky, on earth, in the lakes. The shine is the first sign of
Huracán, the second is the zigzag of lightning, and the third is the thunder
that rolls. And these three are the heart of the sky. It is these who come
to create the world in accord with Gucumatz, the serpent adorned with
feathers.[5]

Given that the majority of our current population is represented by the
indigenous race, one is tempted to confer a nationalist quality to their literature. A number of curious people have studied the surprising number of historical accounts, songs, and poems that our indigenous people treasure. But
inasmuch as this literature is almost ignored by those who do not belong to
the indigenous race or who do not conduct investigations of our indigenous
population, it cannot be called national.

Having seen these false directions and tentative starts in the emergence of
a national literature, we can ask, What will a true nationalist Mexican literature
be like and how can we encourage its emergence?

It is logical to expect that a national literature will appear automatically
when the population is able to unify itself racially, culturally, and linguistically.
By then, the ethical, aesthetic, and religious ideas, the scientific knowledge,
aspirations, and ideals of the distinct groups that make up our population will
have come together and comingled. Our national literature will represent these
diverse origins but have a unified means of expression. When we have fused
culturally, racially, and linguistically, the national soul will be susceptible to
the beauty of that literature, whether it evokes elements of our Spanish, pre-
Hispanic, or colonial heritage.

As a means of collaborating to promote the emergence of this national
literature, we recommend the following.

1. It is of urgent necessity to publish or at least write down that verbal lit-
    erature that we have called "latent"; otherwise, it will continue to decay
    and end up disappearing. This is a task that should be taken up lovingly
    by Mexicans and that has already been initiated by foreign cultural
    centers that interrupted their work during the revolutionary period. It is
    now opportune and patriotic that we pick up this task.

....

[5] For a Spanish edition similar to those that would have been available to Gamio, see
    Adrian Recinos, *Popol Vuh* (Mexico, D.F., Fondo de Cultura Económica, 1960).
    —Trans.

2. The literary works of pre-Hispanic origin that today are almost lost in museums and dusty libraries must be published, since they are fundamentally important for our literary future. Special attention must be conceded to private and official archives that contain documentation from the Colonial period. Also, little-known publications pertinent to the same period must be reprinted.

3. It is necessary to encourage *all* current manifestations of literature, instead of promoting some and inhibiting others. It is foolish to ridicule the little histories of Vanegas Arroyo, the publications of the type of *La Guacamaya*, the touching compositions performed by the troubadors of little plazas, and the stories that emerge from the lips of wet nurses and maids, since all of this is Mexican literature.

4. To work in general for literary dissemination; to edit publications that for their price, for their styles, and for the ideas that they present will be accessible to the greatest number of persons. We think that working in this fashion, we can contribute, at least in part, to the formation of our national literature.

25

Our Women

Nationals and foreigners alike unanimously praise the exceptional virtues of the Mexican woman. We no longer live in the good times when mana fell from heaven to feed the chosen peoples or when the waves of the ocean formed barriers to the passage of their enemies. Thus, we should analyze the natural causes that make our women one of the most appreciable and appreciated moral types in the contemporary female world, instead of seeing her predilections as miraculous.

In any country, there are three classes of women: servile, feminist, and feminine. The servile woman is she who is born and lives only for material labor, pleasure, and maternity—an almost zoological sphere of action imposed on her by the environment. For the feminist woman, pleasure is more sporting than passionate, a peripheral activity and not fundamental. Her characteristics and tendencies are masculine, the home a place of rest and subsistence and a cabinet of work. This type of woman originated and propagated herself profusely in the great centers of population as the logical fruit of that social environment. The feminine woman—a denomination that is somewhat redundant but that is opportune because of its expressive power—is the intermediate woman, equally distanced from the two previous types. This is the ideal woman, generally preferred because she constitutes the primordial factor in the material and intellectual well-being of the individual and the species.

Social science treatises say that the status of woman corresponds to the state of civilization of her country. The more uncultured a people is, the greater the level of servitude; and whilst its culture advances, servitude disappears in equal proportion. According to that sociological conclusion, nearly all Mexican women should be considered servile women, since illiterates constitute 80 percent of our population, and people who would seem uncultured from the European perspective equal 95 percent or more. Nevertheless, this is not the case among us. Although it is true that we have a large number of servile women, they exist in a lesser proportion than would be expected from our apparent lack of culture. Contrary to these expectations, feminine women form a sum that is incomparably greater than that which theoretically corresponds to us, according to the statistics regarding illiteracy and un-culture. Also, the number of truly feminist Mexican women does not correspond in numerical proportion to the population of high culture that inhabits our great urban centers. Her presence is sporadic, exotic, and her numbers infinitesimal. In summary, there are among us fewer servile and feminist women and more feminine women than should exist, given the cultural state that is attributed to our country. To what can we attribute this contradiction of sociological laws that seems to be verified in other countries and societies? We think that there are two motives.

First, it is unjustified that the label of uncultured be applied to Mexico for the sole reason that its civilization is not of the same type as that of the European countries or the United States of North America. This logic is similar to the saying of religious fanatics, "He who is not with my religion is in Hell." Culture is relative, like all else that is humanly known. It should seem antiquated for us to qualify peoples as cultured or uncultured, since we cannot give an absolute value to the term "culture" or "civilization."

Second, the social heritage of the Mexican woman is unique. The contemporary Mexican woman derives her way of being, character, inclinations, and nature from the two women from which she has descended: the Spanish and the indigenous. Had Mexico been conquered by Spain 500 years before it was, the feminine future of our country would have been influenced by enslaved women, by the females without personality that were produced by the dark medieval times. Happily, America surged from the mysteries of the oceans when the last manifestations of the Middle Ages were being extirpated and the glorious times of the Renaissance had begun. These were times when woman, after God, was the supreme symbol of all that was adorable, that was good, that was beautiful. This was the time when the Lauras and the Beatrixes were born into sentimental life, when "For the King and for my Lady" was an obligatory motto for well-born gentlemen. It was this European woman, already dignified by chivalry and civilization, that came to Mexico. Moreover, she was the

Spanish woman, which has been without a doubt the most feminine woman of Europe. We will not insist much on this point, as wise pens have amply exalted the virtues of the woman of Spain.

A. THE AZTEC WOMAN

Let us now evoke the memory of our indigenous mothers and piously live with them for a few instants. In the Mexico of the sixteenth century, there were nomadic and primitive human groups, especially in the north, such as the Yaquis, the Seris, the Coras. But there also existed groups of advanced culture, like the Tarascans, the Zapotecs, the Mayas, and the Aztecs. It is natural that amongst the more primitive tribes, women had scarce social significance, whereas the civilized nations dignified their women with an important role in social organization.

We will consider the Aztec woman as the typical example of the indigenous woman. The importance of the female principle in all creation impressed the mind of the Aztec philosophers as much as it did those of their ancestors, the Teotihuacanos. It was very rare that a physical phenomenon, a material object, or an intellectual activity was not associated with a female deity who accompanied the corresponding male deity. There are cases in which only the female divinity was worshipped. In the last heaven, the highest one, resided the divine couple from which the other gods descended. The oceans, lakes, and currents were reigned over by the "goddess of the skirts of beaded turquoise," who symbolized the blue color of faraway waters. The birth of female creatures was presided over by the goddess Omecihuatl, "double woman" or "two women." According to the opinion of some authors, this name alluded as much to her sex as to that of all female creatures. There was no Cupid or other masculine deity of love in the Aztec Olympus. There were, however, two goddesses: Xochiquetzal, "precious flower," who was the patroness of chaste love, and the old goddess who flew on a broom of reeds and only dealt with carnal relations. Huitzilopoxtli,[1] the true national god, "the most feared and most loved," was born not of a goddess, but of a woman of flesh and blood, a priestess of Coatlán. Among a people that so intensely and profusely deified woman, it is logical that she would occupy a respectable position in the social hierarchy.

The life of the Aztec woman was picturesque and interesting. The birth of female children was presided over, as we have said, by the stone image of the

---

[1] This nonstandard spelling of Huitzilopochtli is in the original.—Trans.

divine "double woman." If the birth was in a poor home, this image was placed close to the mat that was the bed of the laboring woman. In a rich home, the birth was on rich cotton cloths embroidered with great skill. In either case, an altar for offerings and devotions to the goddess would be built to ensure the success of the birth. The midwife, whose knowledge is truly marvelous judged in light of contemporary medical science, placed the newborn in a small crib. Among other rituals, she would put a tiny loom, a distaff, cooking utensils, and other household essentials in the child's little hands, by which it was considered that the future feminine attributes of the little one were consecrated.

In those times, one did not hear of names like Luisa, Mercedes, or Elena, nor were there Sinforosas, Petronilas, or Atenodoras. Names were generally taken from nature, so that a group of these sweet brown-skinned maidens was a living idyll: "precious gem," "little bird taking up flight," "gentle and crystalline current," "fleeting breeze," "perfumed flower." These were all common names in that time.

The personality of the Aztec woman had three aspects derived from three concurrent tendencies of her life: she was a woman of the home, a religious woman, and a social woman. From her mother, she received the strictest moral instruction and the most ample domestic knowledge. She admired the gifts of civic duty and virility in her father, values that made the Aztecs the most powerful pre-Hispanic society of the sixteenth century. These values also explain their voluntary and almost total extermination when the fatherland was thrown under the feet of the Castilians.

The priests inculcated the Aztec woman with faith, hope, and fear, preparing her for a lofty destiny. Chastity was a capital female virtue at that time, even though women of pleasure existed there as they have in all parts. It is known, however, that these were not married women. Monogamy was generalized, since only the *tecutli*, or emperor, and probably some wealthy noblemen maintained concubines and secondary wives. This is no more or less than is done by the sultan in Turkey and by upper dignitaries in Mexico, and privately by any ordinary man who can afford to keep both the "Big" and "Little" houses. Then as today, the husband was the last to know of infidelity. But this was published after it was discovered by any noble or plebeian. Awakening the popular and even national indignation, the poor guilty woman fell beneath inexorable penal law and was mercilessly stoned by the multitude until she breathed her last.

The Aztecs were a people who worshipped cleanliness. The walls of the palaces evoked admiration in the conquerors for appearing "white, brilliant, and polished like sheets of silver." The cleanliness of the men and women was not far behind. It is true that certain rites obliged the priests to avoid contact with water for several seasons, something that was also frequent in the ancient times of the Catholic Church. We should remember that certain Occidental priests and monks thought the same way, and that their sanctity corresponded to the number of "coats of grime" that they had accumulated. It is also notable that the indigenous people who reside in our great urban centers and have come into contact with modern life have forgotten the old hygienic traditions, whereas those who remain in the country persist in their cleanliness.

Our current cuisine owes several delicious dishes to the culinary competence of Aztec women: *mole de guajolote, chilaquiles,* tamales, enchiladas, *manchamanteles,* duck in *pipián,* quesadillas with *cuitlacoche, tortas de ahuahutle, salsa de huacamole, nopales navegantes,* pozole, *tacos de juil . . .* nutritious drinks such as atole, *chile-atole,* chocolate, and others, as well as pulque, whose discovery is traditionally attributed to the famous Xochitl. Feminine manual labor reached great artistic perfection, particularly the embroidery and weavings that are of such beautiful and original designs that they are reproduced today at home and abroad. There were also the famous feather mosaics at the sight of which their Catholic majesties marveled. There were fine palm weavings, by the standards of which today's mats seem crude. These and many other labors occupied the attentions of women, whereas warfare, agricultural tasks, and other properly masculine attributions were left to men.

The education of young Aztec girls was interesting. They did not learn foreign tongues (Tarascan, Maya, etc.) or architecture, or archaeology, or other professions that today we call liberal arts. Instead, they attended the Cuicoyan, a noteworthy official institution that taught fine arts and good manners. There, they were initiated in music; they learned dances and religious and secular songs. At the Cuicoyan, young people of both sexes began to meet each other publicly. There originated friendly relationships and chaste loves that would later be consecrated. Virtuous men were deans of the Cuicoyan. Father Durán and other faithful chroniclers of pre-colonial Mexico are favorably surprised when they refer to the work of this singular academy.

Thus educated, the maidens grew until reaching a determined age, at which they entered the Calmecac (although some authors indicate that this was only for young women of noble birth). This was a dependency of the Great Temple in which they remained for a year to be initiated in the mysteries that they would eventually inculcate in their children, thus preparing themselves for marriage. It appears that some remained in the temple forever, having made a religious devotion.

"For the wedding day," says Orozco y Berra,

they prepared themselves with great rejoicing. The guests arrived at midday, each being given a great deal to eat, flowers and pipes to smoke. Each one of them offered some gift by the fire, depending on their class, with the poorest only giving some maize. Meanwhile, in the house of the bride, she was bathed in the afternoon, her hair was coiffed, she was dressed gallantly. Placing her over a mat close to the home, the elders counseled her on how to fulfill the duties of her new state. A finely crafted matting of many colors was placed near the lighted hearth. Near this was also a vessel of copal, with a few victuals before it. The bride arrived at the door facing the street. The groom emerged to meet her, the two censing each other with braziers in which they put copal. Taking each other by the hand, they entered the hall, seating themselves over the mat with the woman to the left of the man. The mother-in-law of the bride dressed her in a *huipilli*. The mother-in-law of the groom dressed him in a blanket that was knotted over his shoulder. The matchmakers (women officially dedicated to marrying people) tied the blanket of the groom to the *huipilli* (blouse) of the bride. It was a solemn act, the symbol that they would be united in perpetuity. They burned copal (indigenous incense) in honor of the gods. The mother of the groom would wash the mouth of her daughter-in-law and leave her some food, including tamales and mole. The groom put the four first bites of the food into the mouth of his consort, while she would place the second four into his mouth. If they found carbon or ash in the bridal chamber, they would take this as a sign that they would not live a long life, although they would think the opposite if they were to find a grain of corn or some other seed.[2]

Volumes could be written about the Aztec woman, but we think that this will suffice to demonstrate the importance of our pre-colonial feminine antecedents, who have greatly influenced the character and nature of our contemporary women.

B. THE SERVILE WOMAN

The primary thesis of this article is that in Mexico, there are fewer servile and feminist women and more feminine women than there should be given the cultural state attributed to our country. We can demonstrate this with the

[2] The most recent edition of this source is Manuel Orozco y Berra, *Historia Antigua y de la Conquista de Mexico*, ed. Angel Maria Garibay and Miguel Leon Portilla (Mexico, D.F., Porrua).—Trans.

unequivocal statement that there are fewer servile women than should exist in proportion to our illiterate population, because not all illiterate women are servile. Our indigenous women, who form the largest feminine group in Mexico, cannot read or write. But they preserve the great heritage of pre-Columbian habits, tendencies, and education more faithfully than their men do. They are not, therefore, servile but women worthy of consideration by their contemporaries. Naturally, women who descended from women who were servile before the Conquest or who belong to some of the more primitive tribes that we have mentioned before will continue to be servile until their social environment changes. Women today amongst the Lacandónes, Seris, and so forth cannot, in effect, be anything but servants.

The degree of servitude of a woman in Mexico depends more directly on the grade of immorality of her relatives and male relations than on her own illiteracy, race, and social class. The poor maker of tortillas whose pulque-drunk husband favors with two or three daily beatings and the fine lady whose husband is accustomed to force his way into the house full of excuses and cocktails are equally servile. It is notable that when peasant workers—be they indigenous, mestizo, or white—bring their families to our city in search of work, an unfortunate social alchemy makes women who were originally feminine become servile. This happens because of a fatal attraction that the worst aspects of civilization hold for their husbands, who were previously "uncultured." There are women who are slaves to love, slaves to fanaticism, slaves by necessity, and slaves by . . . foolishness, which can be said of Her Majesty Woman with many apologies.

C. THE FEMINIST WOMAN

In Mexico, there are fewer feminist women than would be produced by the sum of the cultured population, which is the most prominent source of feminist women in all countries. Among us, feminism does not appear in direct correspondence to material and intellectual progress or economic competence, as it does in other countries. We consider this exception to be logically explicable and attributable to the nature of our feminine antecedents. The indigenous woman was always servile or feminine. The Spanish woman that arrived in Mexico was always feminine. It is thus logical that our proportion of feminist women be microscopic.

The growing tendency for Mexican women to seek their own well-being in an honest manner when family members are incapable of doing so has erroneously been qualified as a feminist movement. That way of thinking—or, better said, of not thinking—is characteristic of Mexican men who still suffer from a cave-dwelling jealousy. The Mexican woman does not lose her feminine character when she becomes a typist, doctor, lawyer, dentist, or sales clerk. On the contrary, these women should be praised for the fact that as well as remaining feminine, they are willing to confront the sacrifice of intense daily labor. Our deepest respect goes to those little women with such great spirit!

Feminism is not part of a woman's occupation, or of her profession, but something in her character. It should be termed "masculinism," because of the tendency some women have to masculinize themselves in their habits, ideas, aspects, and souls . . . even physically, if it were possible for them to do so. Nor does standing above other women denote feminism. Sor Juana Inez de la Cruz was not only outstanding in regard to other women, illustrious men also envied her talents. She was nonetheless the fifth essence of the feminine. The invincible Corregidora of Querétaro and the heroic Leona Vicario were ideal wives for Domingues and Quintana Roo.

Which, then, are the truly feminist women? A thorny answer . . . it would be preferable to interview a suffragette from London, who would say more in two words than we could in twenty pages. In Mexico, there are very few, which is as much as we can say in our character as slave paladins of our women . . . even of the feminists!

D. THE FEMININE WOMAN

May sculpted arches spring forth, festooned with garlands! May their greatness be proclaimed by golden trumpets and may sonorous silver bells toll! May flowers come to all gardens—the feminine women have arrived! Mothers, wives, sweethearts, sisters, friends are here. We turn our face to see if anything is left in the world and find it deserted! Our mines, timber forests, industries, and schools will bring us progress. But more than any of these, the work of the feminine woman will be the cornerstone and key, the base and crown of the marvelous edifice.

There being, as we have seen, fewer servile and feminist women than naïve sociological laws would seem to dictate for Mexico, it is a positive consequence of arithmetic proof that we must have a higher proportion of feminine women. We have reasoned extensively about the social heritage of the feminine woman, which is the main reason for her statistical predominance today. We will now examine these complementary causes and see which are the current characteristics of the Mexican feminine woman.

What makes our feminine woman so exceptional is her innate aptitude for connecting, for harmonically and fruitfully reforging, characteristics that are either antagonistic or mutually exclusive. She lives at once on earth and in heaven, in the natural and in the artificial, in the material and in the spiritual.

Let us analyze her from a material perspective, coldly and without gallant prejudices. As a wife, she is passionate, exclusivist, more or less jealous. She is an enemy of all artificialism in intimate relations, although always molding herself to the marital sensibilities of her husband. She is instinctively bound to her sacred and transcendent participation in the generation and continuation of life. She is chaste after matrimony, living as modestly as our much-calumniated mother Eve must have lived after having ingested the inoffensive but scandalous apple. She is a faithful observer of the functions that are natural to her sex, without exaggerating, displacing, or forcibly limiting them. This fidelity to nature is evident even in fallen women, for even amongst those poor creatures there are very few who are truly corrupted by deep malice or sexual perversions. This is why foreigners and our own "golden youth" who return home from Paris, France, find them dull and inhibited.

When she is a mother, the feminine woman is an imperial rosette of virtues and qualities, so devoted to her children that she seems connected to them by tangible bonds. Their suffering manifests itself in her body as if they were still at her breast. Sacrifice for her children is no hardship for her—not an obligation, but the supreme joy. She strives to remain healthy, so as to better provide health for her future children. The well-being, strength, physical beauty, and fullness of the life of her children are her chief desire and the primordial object of her concerns. What does this mean in sociological terms? Nothing less than the formation of the individual members of the species, the promotion of a vigorous development that guarantees their future potency. When Mexico is a great nation, it will be for many reasons. But foremost is the creation of a strong, virile, and resistant race, which is now being modeled by the Mexican feminine woman.

Let us now examine her ethics and psychology. How does she see, feel, and express things of the soul, of the heart, and of the intelligence? We will only approach this superficially, for to do otherwise would be like critiquing St. Thomas's *Summa* in half an hour. Our feminine woman does not have an advanced education but knows how to understand life and its accidents, distinguish the good from the bad, the unjust from the just. She promotes what is useful and convenient and places obstacles in the path of that which is prejudicial and noxious. Such a clairvoyant aptitude is a mixture of Indian astuteness and sensibilities that were imported from Spain. The Mexican feminine woman wraps everything in the sweet honey of her great heart—her diplomacy is Christian and not Machiavellic.

The pre-colonial woman was deeply fanatical in her pagan religion. The colonial woman was, as a product of her times, exaggeratedly pious and intolerant. The feminine woman of our own times should be simply pious. Every day she lives closer to the good Christ, who is the wellspring of all love and pardon, than to the hateful Phariseeism that forges curses, excommunications, and cruelty. Is it not better that she has always been closer to religion than to philosophy? Is she not wiser than we are in thinking this way? Is this not the secret of her living happily or in a contented resignation that is only another form of happiness? Is her natural disposition not similar to that philosophical movement toward the sentimental and idealist spheres, which form, in the final analysis, the lintel of the religious world and the essence of the feminine soul?

The Mexican feminine woman does not speculate in the sciences but in souls. Her innate psychological intuition is marvelous but never pedantic. In a glance, she sees the weakest point, the most interesting aspect, the inner truth of different consciousnesses. Unschooled phrenologists have implied that as descendants of indigenes, our women have a reduced mental capacity. They note that their brain weighs a few grams more or less than that of a Hottentot or Parisian and that their facial angle varies by a few degrees or even minutes. That is all empty babble. In the first place, one cannot make scientific generalizations about differences in the brains of women. Second, their brains weigh as much in proportion to the rest of the body as those of men, who until recently had usurped the "trust" of intelligence. Third, it has recently and very sufficiently been proved that the volume and weight of the brain do not significantly influence mental faculties.

Why is it that our feminine woman has so visibly developed that talent called common sense, which captivates us as much as it does the foreigners who have known her up close? We do not pretend to know the answer. This is not the product of her physical heritage, as there is no such thing as the hereditary transmission of mental aptitudes. And so as not to generalize, we cannot forget that there are women who are . . . let us reconcile courtesy and veracity and say "closed in the head."

Poor poets and foreign critics who come from cold countries often dissertate on "tropical Mexican women," the hot blood that runs through their veins, and the flashes of fire that escape from their eyes. They find provocation and voluptuousness in their movement, in their looks, in their laughter, in their voice . . . even in their tears! Such bad poetry! It pleases little and offends much, as it seems like propaganda for the Great Turk to come to Mexico to stock his harems. Those "tropicalist" poets that have just emerged from the icebox of their own countries must be told that they are wrong. The servile woman, especially the indigene, is not truly voluptuous, given her passivity and poorly developed eroticism. The feminine woman feels more but can better measure her passionate instincts insofar as she is better educated than the latter. The feminist woman is not passionate, or perhaps is with an extravagantly masculine aspect. On this matter, we can say nothing more, as we had vowed to say nothing of males in this essay.

That woman who uses her wise and deep instincts to create a family, who constitutes the hopes of the race, in whose heart the idealist paths that lead humanity toward spiritual well-being flower, is the supreme woman. The woman par excellence. Thus is the Mexican feminine woman.

26

. . . .

The National Seal

The adoption of ideographic/symbolic representations that characterize national virtues is one of the oldest of human conventions. A flag and seal synthesize what a nation is or believes itself to be. The colors of a flag symbolize the true virtues of a race: noble valor, honor, purity, hope. The characteristics represented on national seals are more ambiguous virtues. Boldness and even ferocity are proclaimed on almost all national seals: the British and Spanish lions, the Chinese dragon, the Ecuadorian condor, the heraldic eagles of so many countries. All of those bloody images, made in gold and inlays on fields of polychrome silks, are nothing but ancestral vestiges of a time when fearful displays augmented natural aggression and strength. Destruction is also a common motif on national seals, represented by rifles and cannons, swords and lances. The flag is thus more spiritual, more Christian, than the seal.

Our seal has more of a truly national character than those of many other countries. It was forged on the anvil of History with the divine hammer of Fable and the sacred fire of Art. It is at once creative and true, it exists within Beauty and Truth. A beautiful dragon meanders on the Chinese flag, but this dragon has never existed. The lions of Iberia and Great Britain are exotic animals in those countries; they were born in the jungles of Africa and the deserts of Asia. The unicorn of the British arms was invented by some poet or artistking. In contrast, the eagle on our seal is indigenous, not imported. It inhabits the seal legitimately. Those American aesthetes who felt and thought about beauty before the Conquest arrived saw the majestic circling of this imperial bird or saw it perched epically on some spiny bush. From there, they invited

126

that majestic vision to live in their art and in their history, to inhabit the skies of their myths. On our ancient seal, the eagle does not only represent strength and ferocity but also nobility and just power. It is the triumph of what raises itself on high, of the divine, of Good (the eagle) in its eternal struggle against Evil (the serpent).

Unfortunately, more recent representations of our seal have lacked a completely national character. Until the arrival of the Conquest, the eagle and the serpent appeared on jewelry, codices, headdresses, standards, and mural reliefs with the sumptuous originality that characterized pre-Hispanic art. Since then, the seal has transformed into something that looks like a piece of theatre decoration. The eagles on the flags that are sent to us from overseas are not even degraded Napoleonic or Roman eagles but, even worse, mutants painted in detestable colors. Those painted on metal plates that are used by our military have the words "made in Germany"[1] stamped on them.

This sad degradation of our national seal can be attributed to changes and neglect that it suffered in the centuries that came after the Conquest. During the empire of Charles V, and later during that of Maximilian of Hapsburg, eagles stylized in the Austrian fashion were introduced to Mexico. It is notable that this exotic art form traveled to even the last savage corners of Tepic and Jalisco. The Huichol Indians who live there today still decorate their wool and cotton cloth with a two-headed eagle,[2] albeit adapted stylistically to aboriginal tastes. The seal was not a common image during the Colonial period. In the few exceptions when the eagle appears—as an artistic remnant or as a sporadic reappearance—it looks more like a sparrow hawk of Castile than like an Imperial eagle.[3]

The insurgents were glorious and venerable men, but their age was not one of aesthetic flowering, much less so in the case of the national seal. If one looks at the national seals made during this period, it is difficult to say if the bird that so spasmodically flaps its wings is an eagle, a vulture, or a fighting cock. And let us not think that the "aesthetic patriotism" of today has been purified of these older influences. If one examines the eagles printed on official documents, printed on the bills of the bank, or stamped on coins, one sees that they are not beautiful realist works, or conventionalist, or stylized . . . not even cubist. They are not works of art at all but industrial designs, mechanical drawings. These

---

[1]   In the original, this phrase appears in English, as here.—Trans.
[2]   Ethnographic collection of the National Museum.
[3]   Eighteenth-Century Medals and Documents.

are inert eagles without expression or life, secondhand copies of some desiccated original that had already been deformed by termites. In summary, our seal existed in all of its original beauty from fabled antiquity until the arrival of the Conquest. It was abolished for 300 years, after which it reappeared in an exotic, vulgar form.

This sad aesthetic history has two principal causes. First, there is the fact that our modern artistic manifestations have been very poor and lacking in national character. It is well-known that the sumptuous legacy that we received from colonial and pre-Columbian art began to decay in the beginning of the nineteenth century. Second, the composition of our national seal has almost always been executed by craftsmen and not by artists. For lovers of beauty, the craftsman's aesthetic sensibility is simply not convincing.

Before moving to the principal object of this article, we should take into account some zoological, historical, and artistic antecedents of the Mexican eagle. The eagle appears profusely in the art of many of the ancient Mexican families, in spite of the fact that the bird itself only lives in a few states of the republic. In Mexico, there is only one true eagle, known as *Aquila crysaetos* in the Linnaean system, called *cuauhtli* by the Aztecs, royal eagle in common speech, and golden eagle by some naturalists. The interesting work *La Creación* (3:211) gives the following description of this species:

> The golden eagle, *Aquila crysaetos*, is more svelte than the *Fulva* and
> *Imperialis* eagles, as can be observed in the live animal. It has a smaller head
> and longer wings and tail, although the former is not at all covered by the
> latter. The male is 1 meter long with a 2.4-meter wingspan. The female is
> 1.05 by 2.5 meters, respectively. The folded wing measures 0.77 meter and
> the tail measures from 0.36 to 0.4 meter. The adult bird has lighter plumage,
> especially on the chest, buttocks, and underparts of the tail. There is a white
> spot on the small of the back. The tail is a brownish ashy gray, with wide
> transverse back lines distributed irregularly. The terminal waist is narrower
> than in the previous species (*Aquila fulva*). Only the caudal feathers are
> somewhat shortened; the others are of the same length. The inferior part
> of the wing is dark and has no trace of white. Dugés found this eagle in
> Durango, Tower in Guanajuato, and Bullock in more septentrional regions.

The common people think that our seal originated in the remote national past. Better-educated people would probably suggest that it is the symbol of the city of Tenochtitlán, the ancient name of the capital of Mexico. We will cite the following passage from the Geographical Dictionary,[4] one of the most authorized opinions on this topic.

The oldest and most authorized monument that we have of its origin (the seal's) is a hieroglyphic painting that represents the foundation of Mexico, an authentic work of Mexican invention and execution conserved in the first printing of the Mendoza collection (Kingsborough, Antiquities of Mexico, etc., vol. 1) called thus by Antonio de Mendoza. It was discovered on the land that served as the seat for the founders of Mexico, in the way referred to in the entry on Axolohua. The interpreter of the Mendoza codex describes it in the following terms: "At this time there was no water, only large growths of a plant which they call 'tuli' and very large growths of bush, like forests. In all of the space of the settlement they had one source of water that was free of the growths and bush, which had the form of the staff of San Andres, as the figure shows. And almost at the end of this crossroads, the Mexicans found a large stone or deep boulder, on top of which was a large cactus, on top of which a large eagle had its brood and nest, which they could tell because the bones of birds and feathers of various colors filled the space underneath. And this being the origin of the settlement of their population, it was determined by them to call the place Tenochtitlán, because of the cactus grown over the stone."

In my judgment, as in that of many others, the common people are closer to the truth than those who criticize them. It is not the Aztec tribe, founders of Tenochtitlán, who gave origin to the Mexican seal. The composition of the eagle and the serpent, or the eagle by itself, appeared many centuries before in indigenous artwork. We see the same national symbol in the artwork of the earliest villages, the Chalchihuites or transitory art tradition, and the Tarascan, Zapotec, Mayan, and various other art forms that were already in decadent disintegration when the Aztecs had not yet arrived in the Valley of Mexico. Other arguments suggest that the Aztecs brought the fable of the eagle with them from faraway Aztlán as a pretext to establish themselves in new regions. One sees ample proof of the antiquity of this myth in the codices, architectural monuments, ceramics, and all other objects made by the pre-Hispanic families. This is also confirmed by research that has been conducted by authorized modern specialists.[5]

Seler says that the ancient Mexicans distinguished among various different types of eagles, the largest being the *cuauhtli* or the *picigatao* of the Zapotecs. There is also a gray-colored eagle and another one with transverse black lines

____

[4] *Diccionario geográfico, histórico y biográfico de los Estados Unidos Mexicanos,* vol. 1, p. 250, "The Arms of Mexico."

[5] Eduard Seler, "El Aguila" (Der Adler), *Zeitschrift für Ethnologie* 40 (1909): 784.

on a white base that is probably the *itzcuauhtli*. As we have said, there is no other species of eagle in Mexico, so it is probable that the Mexicans considered all hawks, falcons, and similar birds of prey found in all regions of the country to be of the same character.

Artists of forms and ideas who were once thought of as Quixotic on an impossible crusade are today considered to be the precursors of a glorious vernacular renaissance and have attempted to create a national work of art. Would it not be patriotic if those who represent these noble tendencies were to compete for the creation of as important a work of art as is our national seal?[6]

....

[6] This article is an extract of another published in the *Revista de Revistas*, December 5, 1915.

27

Capacity for Work

The question of capital's relationship to labor is debated in most countries, and no one has reached a satisfactory conclusion to date. Recent strikes in the United States, England, and Spain can be cited as a consequence of this difficult problem. The resolution of such problems in Mexico involves even greater difficulties, since the characteristics and historical heritage of our laborers have never been properly studied.

It is indispensable that capitalists know the "capacity for work" of their employees. This is necessary in order to calculate just salaries for those who have just been employed in new businesses and to raise or lower the salaries of those working in established businesses. Our rulers need these data in order to investigate the progress, paralysis, or regression of our productive centers and to estimate the possibilities for industrial, agricultural, or mining production. The capacity for work can be judged in terms of quality and quantity. In each country, there is a typical kind of production that varies according to the nature of the work, the physiographic and biological qualities of the region, and the ethnic, psychic, and economic characteristics of the population.

How can we Mexicans come to know the normal capacity for work of individuals in their various occupations? We must consider their historical antecedents. It is logical that our spinners and weavers, potters, carpenters, saddlers, ropers, and all others who work in pre-colonial and colonial industries are in a position to produce more and better work than those who have a more modern labor experience (such as the makers of mechanical and scientific implements, electric materials, crystal work, and glass).

Few studies have documented how the capacity for labor can be influenced by race. Mexican workers can be divided into two great racial categories, the first comprising individuals of pure Indian race or individuals of mixed race in whom the indigenous component predominates, and the other formed by individuals of original European blood or those in which this blood predominates to a large degree. Those of the first group are slow and moderate generators of energy and effort, but they surpass the second group in terms of consistency, duration, and resistance. It appears that their muscular development is inferior to that of the second group, given that their nutrition is frugal and exclusively vegetarian, being based on corn and its by-products. The workers of the second group can generate greater energies than the first group at any given moment, although for a shorter duration of time. Their muscular development is apparently better and their nutrition more mixed and abundant. Anyone can prove the aforesaid for himself by simply giving the same task to a worker of indigenous race and to another of white race.

The cause that probably motivates the most variations in the capacity for work is the diversity of physiographic conditions in our national territory. That is, the capacity for labor in Mexico has as many variations as there are regions of the republic. In effect, atmospheric pressure, rain, ambient temperature, hygrometric state, and so forth give the cutter of Yucatecan henequen, the guayule cutter of Coahuila, the coffee picker of Cordoba, and other regional workers certain capacities that are adapted to the physical and anatomical characteristics imposed on them by their respective local environments. The capacity for work is also related directly to the economic situation of the working classes and of all of the population in general. To correct the disequilibrium in these capacities, one must either impose a radically socialist sensibility or seek an integral and democratic development that promotes the well-being of workers, bureaucrats, professionals, capitalists, and other elements that make up the national population. In light of this, we suggest that scientific research be conducted privately and by the government. This will allow us to determine the normal capacity for work of Mexican workers, which is absolutely indispensable.

28

Our National Industry

Whether or not we choose to emulate Leroy-Beaulieu,[1] we can examine data on imports and exports in our country and see that our industry is very deficient. We have inexhaustible reserves of the metals that give life to modern industry: iron, copper, lead, antimony. There is an abundance of fuel: wood, charcoal, coal, petroleum, gaseous hydrocarbons. Materials for construction abound: marble, multicolored marble, onyx, polychrome limestones. So do precious materials like gold and silver. We also possess earth for ceramics and glass: red and white clay and silicates, precious stones (pearls, turquoise, emeralds, and opals). Our numerous fibers include henequen, pita, and palm. We have superior meat and skins from wild and domestic animals, rubber and elastics. In short, we have all those things that could make our country one of the foremost industrial producers of the world.

If raw materials are abundant, manual labor competent, and fuel plentiful, what is the cause for the stagnation of our industry? Setting aside the difficulty of transportation and the deficiency of our international mercantile relations, we will focus on factors of even greater transcendence. The fundamental error that limits our industrial potential consists of having inverted the character of industrial production. Rather than promoting national industries and gradually implanting foreign ones, the former were disdained and special attention was given to the latter. As a result, national industry was weakened to the point

----

[1] Pierre Paul Leroy-Beaulieu (1843–1916).—Trans.

of becoming deficient. For the sake of developing a foreign industry, our typical forms of production have been unable to extend and develop themselves. Foreign industry cannot be produced or consumed adequately in our country, given the scarcity of workers who have acquired sufficient experience in foreign centers of industry and the exotic nature of its products. We will consider a more sensible relationship between these two industries in the lines that follow.

A. TYPICAL NATIONAL INDUSTRY

It is of ancient provenience, with roots in the most remote past. Faithful accounts tell us that the court of the Catholic monarchs, a universal emporium of the arts, industries, and sciences, was moved to clamors of admiration at the arrival of objects of indigenous industry from Mexico. Mosaics made of polychrome feathers; mosaics of rich gemstones; amulets and figurines of obsidian, jade, and rock crystal; filigreed jewelry of gold and copper; well-cured skins; and thousands of other things that it would be tiresome to enumerate, all seemed comparable or superior to the products of Europe.

During the Colonial period, European industries were implanted slowly, evolutionarily, until they were fused with indigenous ones. By the end of the eighteenth and the beginning of the nineteenth century, a national industry with many diverse products flourished. An original porcelain was derived from Chinese and Spanish types that were capably interpreted and influenced by the traditional aptitude of Indian ceramicists. In the preparation of skins for saddles, furniture, and weavings, the Moorish knowledge brought by the conquerors and that of the ancient Mexicans were fused. Lacquered objects and furniture made in Mexico competed favorably with the most select of Chinese and Japanese production. Gold and silver filigrees were as beautiful and solidly finished as those made in Italy. Encrustations in metal made Amozoc into the Eibar of Mexico. One could not say if the cloths of Saltillo were more beautiful or durable, and vice versa. The spinning, knitting, and weaving of wool, cotton, and silk; palm and grass weavings; and braidwork were also major industries. These and many other industries made New Spain the foremost industrial emporium of America.

This typical and vigorous national industry would have evolved, fused itself with new foreign industries, and made Mexico into an industrial country had the character of industrial production not been inverted. In effect, when communication with Europe and the United States became easy in the nineteenth century, foreign industries made a profuse appearance. But rather than attempt a fusion between these and our national industries, as the Spanish had done with the indigenous industries after the Conquest, the importers of these new industries sought to annihilate typical production in preference for the foreign. Were it not for the nationalism of the indigenous race and of some other elements of our population that persisted in conserving, reproducing, and consuming the now-decadent national industries, these would have become a thing of the past.

B. INDUSTRY OF FOREIGN CHARACTER

One might expect that foreign industry would have flourished in Mexico in direct proportion to the decadence of typical industry. This did not occur, because the latter is, in spite of its stagnation, more profusely developed than the former. In what foreign industry have we been able to distinguish ourselves, or even reach the normal commercial production that would satisfy the needs and tastes of our population? In very few. We will cite some examples.

In order to give ourselves the luxury of manufacturing Mexican paper, millions of pesos were spent and complicated machinery was installed with the intervention of political and industrial magnates. But in the end, commercial-quality paper could not be made. It is well-known that if foreign paper had not been exaggeratedly and unjustly taxed, it would have annihilated national paper in quantity, price, and quality. There are optimists who say that the production of beer is national. It is easy to demonstrate that this is an erroneous judgment. Our factories make beer with foreign malts, foreign hops, foreign machinery, foreign capital, and foreign technical personnel. This beer is only national because of the land where the factories are situated, the workers who bottle it, and the stomachs that consume it. There are isolated cases in the mechanical industries that denote great competence on the part of our industrialists. One could cite the example of the locomotive on display in the gardens of the Mexican railroad. But unfortunately, this is only a model for what could be made in the future and not the product of normal production.

The production of fine wool and shoes has advanced considerably, with the products being relatively abundant and of good quality. All that is required for the nationalization of this industry is to extend amply the use of shoes and fine wool among the lower classes, who would gradually impose their characteristic tastes on style and production. But this would require a marked improvement of the economic condition of those social classes.

For the sake of brevity, we will not consider any more foreign industries. It is, however, important to note that the products of the foreign industries that have been implanted in Mexico will never pass beyond our borders. It is ridiculous to hope that they can compete with their legitimate counterparts abroad. This is not the case with our typical industries, which have always had open foreign markets as well as national consumption. When will we ever have commercial success delivering fine wool from San Ildefonso to London, shoes from Zetina to Boston, hats from Tardan to New York, beer from Toluca to Munich, and rails from Monterrey to Pittsburgh or Le Creusot? On the other hand, palm and straw hats and mats, ceramics, cloths decorated with colonial or pre-Hispanic motifs, gold and silver filigree, and innumerable other objects of our typical industry can be sent to foreign markets, where they compete favorably in price and quality and carry the stamp of their indisputable authenticity. Some time ago, when notable foreign industrialists came to Mexico, we sought their sincere opinion regarding our industrial production. They unanimously find our typical industries to be very interesting and see our foreign-type industries as poor caricatures. They state that the former would find an ample market abroad, but the latter would not be taken into consideration.

C. THE TRUE NATIONAL INDUSTRY

In our country, where the political environment is biting and irony is a chronic affliction, one has to look backward in order to move forward. Let what has been said here not be misinterpreted. Let no one say that, like old women of the sacristy, we condemn modern scientific industry sent to us from France, Germany, or Belgium. Nor should we preach a ridiculous industrial nationalization that would make us prefer the *trajineras*[2] of Santa Anita to gasoline boats, colonial chests to Mosler strongboxes, the signal horn of the Zapatistas to the wireless telegraph, the horse-drawn *volan-coché*[3] of Yucatán to the rapid Fiat. Far from it, we hope that foreign industry will be implanted profusely in Mexico. However, this should never replace or create obstacles to the formation of a truly national industry from the evolutionary fusion of the foreign and the typical. We propose that, first, we dispose of or limit the ridiculous exotic tendencies that make us unconditionally prefer foreign types of industry to the typical. Second, we promote the production of typical industry to increase

----

[2] Small, flat-bottomed boats.—Trans.
[3] A light, large-wheeled wagon or buggy.—Trans.

its consumption in our country and satisfy and augment the demand that has always existed for it abroad. Third, we apply the techno-methodology of foreign industry to our typical industries and work toward the fusion that came about so spontaneously and brilliantly during the Colonial period. Fourth, we send our workers to foreign industrial centers, so that they may incorporate foreign experiences to their traditional industrial aptitude. Fifth, we establish expositions of typical Mexican products in foreign countries and exhibitions of new and unknown foreign industries in Mexico. Having done this, we can applaud the fact that many new foreign industries will be implanted in Mexico, as we will be apt to comprehend, reproduce, and nationalize them.

29

Of Yankee and Mexican Metalism

We call the United States the Country of the Dollar. Ironically, these words do not refer to the proverbial wealth of that republic but to the way of being of its inhabitants, whose goals in life we unjustly consider to be unspiritual, utilitarian, and materialist—"metallized" to the exclusion of any altruistic motive. Were other countries to qualify the United States in this way, it would still be an exaggeration. It might even be forgiven if those critics had virtues that those whom they criticize do not. But we should remember the proverb about the splinter in the neighbor's eye, because it must be understood that we Mexicans are much more materialist and metallized than our neighbors, the Yankees. Sadder still, we are able to pile up no more than mounds of cents, whereas the children of the "country of the dollar" pile up mountains of dollars.

We will try to demonstrate this, ignoring the accusations of anti-patriotism that will be applied to us by patriots with Quaternary sensibilities, by poor and backward men who would be proud of their homeland because it is the greatest producer of pulque. Given that European civilization established itself in Mexico 200 years before it did in the United States, it would be expected that our culture would be as ample and intense as those of the North Americans. But what occurs is exactly to the contrary. Whereas the United States boasts an advanced stage of culture, we[1] vacillate between childhood and adolescence, or have not yet been weaned, as is the case with our many illiterates. This, like all

[1]   We refer here exclusively to the Mexican population of European origin.

phenomena of the social order, has various and very complex causes, of which we will only mention a few.

From the beginning of the Colonial period until the present day, we have never dedicated ourselves to works of culture. Rather, our activities have gone toward the satisfaction of material needs, to the vain luxury of accumulating wealth. We live behind our business, our "job"[2] or the post that gives us money to feed our needs, vanity, or avarice. Our failure has been complete, since we have developed neither enviable manifestations of culture nor the wealth that one would expect given our utilitarianism and metallism.

The people of the United States pursue the dollar tenaciously, forgetting all else. But once they possess it, they use a respectable proportion of it to create, sustain, and promote works for culture and for humanity. Rockefeller has earned millions upon millions of dollars by extorting the people but in exchange has transformed fifty or a hundred of those millions into a scientific institute. At the Rockefeller Institute, there is constant work to better the conditions of humanity. There, Carrel[3] studies the mysteries of biology, lifesaving serums are cultivated, other scholars explore new applications for electricity or perfect new agricultural applications. There are a hundred, a thousand centers like this one in the United States. Great universities, scientific institutes, hospitals, and so forth have been created and sustained by the altruism of the hunters of the dollar, by the "metallized" people whose dryness of the soul we are so pleased to criticize.

We—with the exception of one for every thousand—hoard our money. The more we make, the stingier and greedier we become. Money is spent on luxuries but never to promote the advancement of our culture or to secure our social well-being. When have our magnates disinterestedly founded schools, research institutions, art academies? Never! Is it not entirely shameful that when there was no official aid for the maintenance of schools in this capital during the Zapatista interregnum, society did not come together en masse to provide the aid that was missing?

And do not think that we only fault men from wealthy backgrounds, because we all share the blame. Our lawyers, doctors, engineers, architects, and other professionals who are not exactly wealthy carry their titles like a banner

---

2   Quotation marks in original ("chamba").—Trans.

3   Alexis Carrel (1873–1944), a biologist with controversial links to the eugenics movement.—Trans.

in the fight for the peso. One can literally say that they exchange the knowl-edge that they have acquired for money. They are content to do what they were taught to do and do not try to augment their knowledge unless the attempt is profitable. They do not give a disinterested grain of sand for the advancement of the science or sciences that they study. They exploit their profession rather than cultivate knowledge. In the United States, professionals also tend to earn money. But in exchange, they conduct research and perfect themselves in the science of their profession for the sake of the science itself. We could mention the hundreds of American professionals who have made transcendent innova-tions in medicine, engineering, law, philosophy, and so forth. The same cannot be said of Mexican professionals, except with very rare exceptions.

Of course, it should be understood that the problems that we have pre-sented here are less the fault of individuals than the environment and circum-stances that surround them. However, that alone will not pardon the fact that we erroneously brand the Americans as utilitarian and metallized now that we are those things to a greater degree.

30

Spain and the Spanish

Author's note: this article was written some months ago.

I do not suffer from acute Hispanophilia. I do not come to defend Spain or her children, who do not lack pens or brains that would let them do so themselves. I am a Mexicanist. I began doing works for nationalism some time ago, and continue to do so. I am beyond suspicion. Therefore, I speak to all for the sake of our faulty common sense. Why, O why are there people who persecute the Spanish systematically, unjustly, and unnecessarily? People who declare that this Spaniard over here, and that one and that one over there, and all Spaniards everywhere deserve to be hanged or even burned at the stake?

One should not attack nationalities, but individuals. Let it be said, if it be the case, that "gachupin X is a thief" or that "H fled from Ceurta." But let no one commit the cowardly crime of insulting the Spanish every time that he has a toothache or is bitten by an insect. We should ask ourselves in good faith if it is necessary to renege on our kinship with the Spanish. Among us there are patriots who are ill with ignorance and "pre-Hispanic tricolorism," perhaps descendants of Cacamatzin, Topiltzin, or some other "tzin," who deplore the Conquest of Mexico. They wish that it had never happened, supposing that our country would now be a powerful indigenous nation like Japan. Those who think this way live in limbo, because it is infantile to think that Mexico could have existed forever without being discovered. Had it not been Christopher, other Columbuses would surely have come forth. Had its geographic virginity been prolonged until today, our nation would be as ripe to fall into the hands of the first conqueror as it was in 1521. All of its notable achievements would not be sufficient to defend it from the strength of others.

If our being conquered was unavoidable, we should ask what our destiny might have been if a nation other than Spain had subjugated us. Only after clarifying this point can we know whether to curse or be grateful for the destiny that put us in the hands of Ferdinand and Isabel. Three nations could conceivably have conquered us at that time: France, England, and Portugal. There are those who would say Holland as well, but that will not be considered here. We would not have lasted as a French colony. We would have been sold to the United States more than a century ago, as was done with Louisiana. Otherwise, the Americans would have taken us by force. It is well-known that the pioneer's way of colonizing was more radical than that of the Spanish conquerors, as it consisted of exterminating the Indian population, so that now even the marrow of our country would be Yankee. Just thinking about this should make Mexicans angry, even the Hispanophobes.

Had the English lion sunk its claws into Mexican soil, two possibilities could have occurred: either we would have been independent in the eighteenth century as an integral part of the United States or perhaps we would still be under British rule. The British would undoubtedly respect our customs, religion, and so forth, but not our sovereignty. We would live like the people of Belize, ethnically and nationally hybrid. Is it not better to be free with the vices of Spain than slaves with the virtues of England?

We are left with Portugal. We have nothing but respect and admiration for the compatriots of Camoens and their brilliant national history. But frankly, we think that Spain has been superior to Portugal in art, science, industry, and wealth over the course of the centuries. Colonized by Portugal, we would be less than we are today, although perhaps more arrogant.

If, then, being conquered by any of those three nations would not have made us happier or less disgraced than Spain did, we are left with few options. Perhaps we can consider how our national life would be today if we had been conquered by the Martians or by Nietzsche's supermen. Let Spain be absolved of the original sin of the Conquest.

This much regards the Spain that conquered us. We will now see if it is right to guillotine her sons, the Spaniards who live with us today.

A. THE QUESTION OF RACE

Economists, sociologists, ethnologists, and other knowledgeable men have often said that the redemption of Mexico will only be reached through foreign immigration. Supposing that this very debatable assertion were true, one should ask, What immigrants should be brought in order to avoid the failures of past attempts? Germans, Englishmen, Frenchmen, Italians, and other foreigners arrive in the country speaking exotic languages and, after amassing a fortune, take it back with them to their country of origin. These foreigners only ever cross their blood with women of the upper or middle class and never, or almost never, with indigenous women. This does not make them into ideal immigrants (now that the Mexican population of Indian blood is the majority), given their prejudice in considering the indigenous race to be inferior. The Spanish, on the other hand, have not disdained to cross their blood with ours, from Cortés to the present day. Whom should we esteem more? The cultured, civilized, ultramodern people who nonetheless look upon us with the protective air of disdain that is conceded to intelligent apes in a circus? Or those who are perhaps less advanced but who consider us humanely and do not fear to cross their blood with ours?

B. THE ECONOMIC QUESTION

We will not comment on the laboriousness of the Spaniard; any wag could imagine that our praise of them is moved by gachupin pesetas. We will simply criticize them justly. There is a group of Spaniards who has profited in a way that is truly disagreeable for us Mexicans, and offensive and prejudicial for their own compatriots. We refer to the swindlers, the very reason why Hidalgo's cry of "death to the gachupins" has been transmitted from generation to generation in our country. The pawnbroker, the usurer, the dealer in misery is the man most hated by the people of all countries. This is the deep cause of the popular hatred, which is the worst of all hatreds.

Labor recruiters, hacienda owners, and enslavers of Spanish nationality do exist and must be annihilated. But it cannot be denied that these vices exist in equal proportion among Mexicans and the other groups of foreigners. Had things been otherwise, it would have been enough for the revolution to extinguish only the Spaniards in order to turn Mexico into a paradisiacal garden.

C. THE POLITICAL QUESTION

We detest filibustering by any nationality. Some nameless, half-starved Spaniards had affiliated themselves with the previous governments of this country, a collaboration that is the cause of the eternal clichés of "busybody gachupins" and "scoundrels." At the same time, we know of Americans, Germans, and

Frenchmen that also intervened in our public affairs. We never vilified all of their compatriots living in Mexico, much less the entirety of the nations from which they hailed. Is it that the armor, the cannons, the strength of the countries where those gentlemen were born lighten our anger against them?

The new state of affairs in Mexico should bring justice to all. In the name of justice, the Spaniard should be viewed through the same prism as other foreigners, if not always with the affection that our close kinship seems to demand. But perhaps that affection could be considered sentimentalism, and we are not dealing with issues of the heart here but of thought. So let there be health and respect to the Spaniards, and let us enforce the thirty-third article of the constitution[1] to the gachupins, who are the Spaniards abandoned by the hand of God.

....

[1] This is a reference to the thirty-third article of the 1857 Constitution, which was still the law of the land when *Forjando Patria* was written. The article refers to the rights of foreign citizens, their subjection to Mexican law while in national territory, and the responsibility of the government to "expel pernicious foreigners."—Trans.

31

Integral Education

It has often been preached that our national well-being and the greatness of the *patria* depend on the literacy of all Mexicans. However, we do not believe that education can produce such miracles if it is not accompanied by other complementary factors, such as the political, economic, and ethnic fusion to which we refer in this book. The isolated injections of literacy that have until now been applied to the Mexican population have been almost useless, because parallel attention was not conceded to the superior stages of education. One should only ask the thousands of our countrymen who have learned to read if that knowledge in and of itself gives them all the well-being that they have wished for. To further demonstrate this point, we should use statistical observations to determine if the prosperity of different regions of the country is related directly or inversely to alphabetization.

In order for the cultural evolution of a people to be normal, it is indispensable that all of the elements that constitute the population be educated in a way that was appropriate for their own ethnic and cultural antecedents. This can only be attained through the implantation of integral education. For example, the high grade of evolution that France and Germany have reached in their manifestations of culture is the result of the systems of integral education that were imposed in those countries in the beginning of the nineteenth century by illustrious thinkers such as Napoleon and von Humboldt. If our population were racially homogeneous and possessed a common language and the same tendencies and aspirations, it would be easy to adopt an educational plan such as those that have been successful in other nations. Unfortunately, the heterogeneity of our population, the multiplicity of our languages, and the divergences in our modalities of thought make such an implantation impossible.

Should integral education be implanted in Mexico? one asks after noting an apparent contradiction in the previous lines. Yes, it should be implanted, but only with a previous and solid knowledge of the population. Let us briefly examine what has been done in Mexico to this end and explore what more could be done.

Education in Mexico suffers from a very general lack of integration. Many of our formerly illiterate countrymen were taught how to read and write but not to use their knowledge of reading in any way that has practical implications for their intellectual and material life. The possession of the alphabet did not help them to alleviate their hunger, or to elevate their ideas. Likewise, the successful professionals that emerge in Mexico are, with few exceptions, mere machines for making money. Our institutions do not train researchers to make original contributions to the scientific progress that is the basis of human wellbeing. The pedagogical colleges happily gestated and birthed teachers blessed by the ideas of Pestalozzi and Froebel.[1] But these teachers have only been able to emancipate the small minority of illiterates whose environment and ethnic antecedents make them apt to receive a European type of education. The brains of the majority of our population remain trapped in the shadows. They beg loudly to be educated not with the European type of pedagogy but in accordance with their historical antecedents and the conditions of the medium in which they live today.

We must adopt a new orientation for the implantation of an integral and nationalist education. This entails that:

1. We need to augment the university's funds considerably, so that the professors who will mold the teachers of the teachers and the teachers of the professionals will be of greater number and competence. It is especially urgent to produce anthropologists, biologists, historians, psychologists, and sociologists, because it would be impossible to begin developing integral education without their input.

2. We must allow centers for scientific investigations, such as the Pasteur, Rockefeller,[2] and Carnegie institutes, to be established in Mexico with

---

[1] Johann Heinrich Pestalozzi (1746–1827), Friedrich Fröbel (1782–1852); classic figures in pedagogical theory.—Trans.

[2] Spelled Roquefelle in original.—Trans.

private or public funds, so that our studied men can dedicate themselves to such speculations as they feel inclined.

3. We must make special departments to form teachers for the indigenous population in our pedagogical colleges. These teachers must be taught by competent ethnologists, these being the people who best know the indigenous population and its needs.

4. An inexpensive, elemental, practical, and utilitarian education must be developed at all costs and in all of the republic.

When the previous suggestions are added to what has already been done to advance integral education, the cultural evolution of the country will proceed normally, efficiently, and evenly.

32

The Editorial Department

In Mexico, there are readers who are apt for the most ample and select literary production, be it European, North American, or Mexican. There is also a disappointing majority that ignores the alphabet. This apparent anomaly could be explained in many ways, but we will refer the following lines to the lack of literary dissemination that has always been notable among us. We have often heard individuals who have recently learned to read say that their hard-won knowledge has proved to be impractical and useless to them. When, for lack of books, one cannot read anything more advanced than the syllabary or the reading book, knowledge of the alphabet seems pointless and unproductive.

Unfortunately, there is no other recourse for the majority of Mexicans who learn how to read, since very few are able to receive a more extensive education or to obtain printings of any other genre. Pamphlets, books, and publications in general have always been a costly article in Mexico and one little suited to the diverse sensibilities of the population. This problem has been ameliorated, albeit deficiently, for the intellectual "elite," who can pay for what they read, and for the children of the urban schools, who are given textbooks. But what of the rest, the great mass that hopes to treasure knowledge through reading? Are they not worthy of attention?

To face this problem, the Bureau of Public Instruction and Fine Arts has proceeded to create an editorial department that will have the dissemination of human knowledge as its lofty goal. They are editing books, pamphlets, and periodical publications that will be priced within the reach of the majority of the population and that will give lessons with practical and efficient results.

This department will also attend to the needs of the intellectual "elite" and to the school-age children. Given the nationalistic and democratic principles of the revolution, all social classes and groups should receive the cultural benefits that correspond to their particular conditions and aptitudes. Now, the Indian who struggled to learn how to write in the poor schools of the mountains and has nothing to amplify his rudimentary knowledge other than his syllabary can acquire elemental and utilitarian texts at an insignificant price. These would give him objective facts about the fields in which he lives, the way of planting and cultivating them, and the wild and domesticated animals of the region. He could also learn of the notable men and salient deeds of the past, and so on. For his part, the laborer of the cities will find works with qualified advice on how to excel in his industry, on how to obtain greater output from it, on simple hygienic rules to improve his health and that of his family, on civil and social instruction to fortify his sense of community, and so forth.

The lover of belles lettres will be able to delve into all of the literature written here and overseas, without sacrificing his pocketbook to the prejudice of more urgent needs. The little ones of the primary school, the preparatory school, and professional students will find countless benefits from this most noble institution. Perhaps Jewish editors will launch a scream into the air when the editorial department begins to function.[1] But there should be no reason for such laments. Given that the editorial department will promote a passion for education and reading in all of the population, its own production will not suffice to meet our needs. The reading public will inevitably turn to other editors, who would grow to greater numbers than today, although now selling their products at the reasonable prices imposed by competition.

The editorial department also has another very important object, which is to stimulate national literary production. Literature is understood here in its widest definition. That is to say, it comprehends everything that is written on whatever subject. Up until today, Mexican authors have had to follow a painful pilgrimage so that their texts would be edited—and under very poor conditions at that. Besides the fact that the profits generated by these works were extremely small, they were not promoted with proper advertisement. Books are sold mechanically and almost always limited to the capital. From now on,

----

[1] I have not determined who exactly is the target of this seemingly anti-Semitic remark. However, it may be a reference to members of European Jewish families who immigrated to Mexico in the 1880s and whom Gamio's contemporaries may have associated with the intellectual elite of the Porfiriato.—Trans.

the department will edit unedited works that a competent and dispassionate jury deems worthy of being published. It will immediately make the necessary promotion in the country and abroad. Lastly, the cost of the raw material and labor will be scrupulously drawn from the final product of the edition, with the rest being given to the author. When it is deemed necessary, works will be edited for free.

The editorial department offers other interesting aspects, but this article would become too long if we were to discuss them all. However, it could be said that this department is among the most transcendent innovations that the revolution has brought to Mexico.

33

Revolution

Revolution is not, as it was considered by medieval Catholics, a divine scourge. Nor is it the favorite means of propaganda that Satan has adopted in our times. These characterizations might be applied in the European context, where the number of victims is infinitely greater and where the means of extermination are more modern, numerous, and efficient. Revolution does not represent the vengeful arm of God that purges the gangrene and corruptions of dictatorships and tyrannies. Let us respect divinity and not attribute to it any role in the destruction of human creatures that wars and revolutions bring with them. The wars propagated by the human species are indifferent to God and even repulsive to Him. In spite of the countless pleas that have been made to Him for peace, wars and revolutions and the consequent sacrifice of lives have taken place without interruption and with growing intensity from the beginning of the world until our times.

Let us then judge the revolution from a purely human perspective. From this perspective, we do not believe that the revolution hates, or should hate, its so-called political enemies. Nor should these hate the revolution. The historical antecedents that made the revolution inevitable are far older than any of its living protagonists. The Conquest and the character of Spanish domination motivated a series of unfavorable social phenomena in our country: inequality between social classes, racial heterogeneity, differences in languages, and divergence or antagonism in cultural tendencies. These phenomena became obstacles to national unity and to the embodiment of a *patria* that would bring about and preserve our general well-being. The current revolution and all of the others that have occurred during our independent life have been nothing else but attempts to transform these unfavorable phenomena into something favorable to national development.

Is it sensible to attribute the social suffering that the revolution has inevitably brought with it to the revolutionaries themselves? Is it sensible to attribute the social sufferings of the past to the dictators that ruled at that time? It is not sensible to attribute culpability in either case, as the roots of both lie in the distant past. Nor should one take this argument as an excuse to curse the Conquest, Spain, and her sons. As we have shown in the article titled "Spain and the Spaniards," our pains would probably be deeper had we been conquered and colonized by another nation.

Who, then, bears the weight of our blame? it could be asked. No one, because it is not a matter of guilt. Who does one blame for the disgraces caused by an earthquake, a flood, or a tempest? Likewise, no one is guilty of murdering the victims of a revolution that emerges from centuries-old social processes.

Then, why fight? Why produce suffering in our peers, if the march of societies is ruled by laws as immutable as those that rule matter? one could reply. To this we say that one has to fight, with all of our weapons and all of our ideas, as one fights against the elements. We must take advantage of those immutable laws and not oppose ourselves to their consummation. If torrents fall from a mountain and inundate our houses or our fields, it would not be worthwhile to destroy the torrent or the mountain, but to take advantage of them. One channels the water and sunders and perforates the mountain, obtaining motor force that can be used for our benefit. One proceeds in a similar way with societies. Without revolution, for example, it would be impossible to annihilate the social elements that governed us during the administration of General Díaz. The revolution is pushing aside the obstacles that oppose themselves to the well-being of the majority of the population. The revolution makes transcendent contributions to the creation of the future nationality and the emergence of the future Mexican *patria*. The individuals and social classes that have created the aforementioned obstacles, or that generate them indirectly, need to separate and transform themselves of their own volition or be separated and transformed by the revolutionary movement.

Those who in actuality or imagination found that their personal interests were harmed by the revolution and who now create obstacles for the revolution rather than facilitate its march work against their own well-being. As they place more obstacles before the revolutionary movement, this movement becomes deeper and more radical. The first period of the revolution, known as the Madero period, offers us a palpable example of this phenomenon. Various factions sought to impose barriers against the revolutionary torrent, beginning with the impolitical action of Ciudad Juarez. The lukewarmness, the wavering, the weaknesses of those who led the revolution at that time, along with the resistance and open hostility of their enemies, produced an apparent paralysis, a momentary dulling of the revolution. Through noisy and initially futile protests, the revolution accumulated energies and brewed with indignation and anger. When that fatal moment arrived and elements of the old regime thought that the revolution could be killed by assassinating Madero, it resurged more vigorous, more deeply rooted, and more radical than before. Those who had been hostile to the revolution during the first period because it did not smile at or court them were harshly punished in this second period. Now they do not strive for smiles but simply for fewer lashes.

The current radicalism could be greater, much greater, if the progress of the revolution were hindered. The revolution must be considered as a natural happening, completely natural. One must march with it, not against it. Placing obstacles in its path would be like trying to immobilize the ocean or darken the day.

34

Three Nationalist Problems

Three nationalist problems deserve special mention because of their current importance and future transcendence, even if they pass unperceived by the masses.

A. THE MAYAS OF QUINTANA ROO: CALLED SAVAGE INDIANS

The Mayas of Quintana Roo, like the Lacandónes of Chiapas, the Maya of the Petén, and a few other groups that are called savages, are indigenous people that live in almost the same state in which their ancestors were surprised by the Conquest. They have never known Spanish or any aspect of the civilization imported from Europe. They have only assimilated the use of firearms, iron utensils, and alcohol. This last factor is a sad legacy that surely makes their lives today more painful than before the coming of the white man. These Indians live off the hunt and the corn that they plant; they worship their mountains, their rivers, their valleys, and their brilliant skies. Their patriotic sentiment is limited to love for their women, for their children, and for their own lives of freedom. These men have justly insisted, from the times of Cortés and Montejo until the present day, that they be permitted to live in tranquility in the territory that they have held for so many centuries.

New Spain was immense, and the mutilated republic[1] still is. Thousands of square kilometers are still unexploited. There was, and still is, enough for

---

[1] This is a reference to the reduction of the size of Mexico in 1848. Before the Mexican-American War, the landmass of the republic had been nearly contiguous with that of New Spain.—Trans.

all. However, under the governments of all of the viceroys and all of the rulers of independent Mexico, the primitive creatures of which we speak were persecuted by the greed of private citizens and politicians. Bad governments fought against them and ultimately sought their extermination. Through the centuries of bloody conflict, the outnumbered Indians never ceded. They have abandoned some territories that then passed into the hands of the whites, but they still occupy extensive lands in which there is no law beyond that which they dictate.

These are Indians of pure blood. They have, until today, succeeded in fleeing from contact with the whites and live undisturbed, thanks to their warlike nature and the geographic isolation of the territories that they occupy. They have their own language and their own culture. Numerically, they constitute a barely noticeable minority compared with the totality of the national population.

Several of these primitive tribes, represented by their patriarch, their priest, or general (we do not know for certain what functions the supreme authority exercises among them), addressed themselves to the government of the triumphant revolution. They declared something that they have repeated for four centuries: they do not want to harm the whites, but they do not want to be harmed by them. They asked that they be allowed to live according to their own customs in the territories that are legitimately theirs. These are sensible desires that seem to be torn from the tablets of the Ten Commandments or from the parables of the Sermon on the Mount. The revolution, with deeds rather than with words, opened its heart to these just petitions and ordered its soldiers to solemnly respect the territory of those tribes and not interfere in their free existence. Because of these just actions, we have seen an extraordinary phenomenon. The indigenous people of Quintana Roo, who had lived in eternal struggle with the whites, now live and work more peacefully than the inhabitants of some of the more civilized regions of the republic.

Today, we can think more carefully about the revolution's future course of action. We can ask, That liberty, the isolation that has been conceded to those indigenous people, is it temporary or definitive? Is it sensible to leave those creatures abandoned to a system of life that, as legitimate as it might be for them, retards the ethnic, cultural, and linguistic fusion of the national population? Why deceive ourselves, if the revolution was not meant to deceive?

It is an irrefutable fact that the indigenous people whom we are discussing have a sacred right to the way in which they have developed and to continue to enjoy the free existence that they have always lived. But it is also an irrefutable fact that the other groups that form the population of the republic have the legitimate right to avoid the collective harm brought by the material isolation and cultural divergence of these smaller groups. From these two antagonistic rights, a mutually favorable conclusion can be deduced: while the revolution tries to solve problems of greater urgency, it should allow the indigenous groups like those of Quintana Roo to exist freely, as it has done. Afterward, it will be necessary to come to know those Indians, investigate their necessities, and establish the conditions in which their incorporation into national society can begin, always making sure that this incorporation is equally beneficial to all and not just to the parties of white race.

It is, of course, important that the study of these Indians not be commissioned to military men, merchants, agriculturalists—as was mistakenly done during the Colonial period and in the nineteenth century—but to specialists who know the regional language and are apt to investigate the indigenous mentality. The few faithful descriptions that we have of the nature and way of life of these Indians have come from specialists, mostly foreign ethnologists, who were received by them with a sense of peace and friendship. All others who have tried to deceive the good faith of those so-called savages have reddened the hard soil of our tropical lands with their own blood. Therefore, we must begin training those specialists today or bring in foreigners, or resign ourselves to the fact that the prejudicial and harmful situations of the past will continue.

It can be guessed—since we do not have sufficient data—that the indigenous population represented by the groups we have discussed sum up to more or less 10 percent of the whole population of the republic.

B. YAQUI INDIANS: CALLED SEMI-CIVILIZED

These people are also of pure indigenous race and are represented by a number of similar groups: Tepehuanes, Tarahumaras, Huicholes, and so forth. They have had more ample contact with the white man than the groups described above. As a result, they know the advantages and disadvantages that this contact brings with it far better than the savage Indians. This contact has often been fatal to them. Just glancing at any historical text, we can see that they have been engaged in bloody fighting for their well-being from the day that they began to be conquered until the present day. One of these groups is at war today, the other tomorrow, but always one or the other. These men have never had anyone to defend their rights before the civilized men who exercise power. As soon as one of these Indians becomes incorporated into civilization, he forgets his brothers or even fights against them. Who amongst the whites has ever sought to get to know them, besides a few scientists who weigh nothing in the political balance? Because of this, these Indians have obtained better results from defending their rights with the barrel of the rifle or the edge of a machete, which is the most rational argument that can be made by someone who cannot count on justice.

These indigenous people could not avoid contact with whites, being forced into it by the geographic situation of the territory that they occupy. They agreed to live under the supreme authority of men who represented another race and who possessed different ideas, but insisted that the dispossession of their lands stop. They also asked that they be permitted to choose their own ruler in internal matters, to be led by someone chosen from among their own race, someone who knows their needs and aspirations. The revolution accepted the general form of the proposal and has been able to prove its commitment to these indigenous groups on several occasions. One need only ask any of our military leaders about the anonymously heroic role that an indigenous soldier of this affiliation played in the revolution.

There is a case that deserves special attention, that of the indigenous people of Xcanha (Campeche). These Indians can be included in the same group as the Yaquis, Huicholes, and so forth. They asked the governor of that state for the same thing that has been requested by many similar groups in other parts of the republic: autonomy in local government in exchange for recognizing and supporting the authority of the governor and the chief of the nation. These conditions were accepted and solemnly maintained by both parties. A few months later, those indigenes of the "Republic of Xcanha" (as it was jokingly known in the region) surprised a party of counterrevolutionaries. Remembering their sacred pact, they captured them and turned them over to the authorities without pomp or expectations of compensation. Is this not a good example of the transcendent results brought about by the observation of justice, mutual esteem, and respect between dissimilar elements of the population?

By what means can we promote the incorporation of these Indians, who undoubtedly pose less resistance than those of the previous group? We must begin by securing their rights to the lands that they currently occupy and by returning the lands that were once torn away from them. This task has already been begun by the revolution. At the same time, we must strive for their physical, economic, and intellectual development. This should not, of course, imply that their original culture be annihilated through the brusque imposition of other cultural ideas. This would be neither possible, nor fair, nor sensible. On the contrary, we should facilitate the spontaneous development of their culture and collaborate in the evolutionary fusion of this culture with the culture of the race that has been dominant until now. Looking at the republic to our north, can we not see that the habits, ideas, and race of 200,000 indigenes develop with complete freedom amidst the 100 million North Americans who manifest a culture of European origin? This is because the old sensibility that "the only good Indian is a dead Indian" no longer predominates in the United States. Rather, a scientific sensibility preaches respect for Indian life, studies it consciously, and helps to promote its normal development. We repeat that this indigenous population only constitutes one fourth of 1 percent of the total population of the United States. Nevertheless, there exist numerous public and private institutions that promote their conservation and betterment, always respecting their particular history and the evolution of their original civilization. In sad contrast, the indigenous population represents a majority in Mexico, but the leadership of our country has always viewed them with distrust, fear, and condescension.

C. THE POPULATION OF MORELOS

Does the Zapatismo of Morelos only represent banditry and pillage or does it embody a people's tenacious hopes for well-being and freedom? We shall first define and delimit three distinct aspects of Zapatismo. The first of these is simple banditry, which in Morelos, as in other parts of the republic, often hides behind the face of revolution. Second, there are surviving elements of the previous regime that have taken advantage of the eternal disorientation of the Indian and sent him off on nefarious adventures. Lastly, there is the legitimate Zapatismo, which could better be called Indianism. Zapatismo is a localist and temporary denomination that is bound to disappear, whereas Indianism has persisted vigorously in Mexico since Cortés placed his standard on the sands of Villa Rica.

For acts of banditry committed in the name of Zapatismo, the revolution has resolved to employ the medium used in all times and all places for the same purpose: extermination without mercy. For the reactionary elements of Zapatismo, the revolution seeks to combat them correctively, keeping in mind that these misguided Indians are simply mechanical instruments that are pushed and directed by remnants of the former regime that are currently living in exile or in other parts of the republic. When this reactionary leadership is annihilated, reactionary Zapatismo will disappear automatically.

All that is left is to analyze the legitimate Zapatismo, which we have called Indianism. The population of Morelos is representative of indigenous groups of pure and mixed blood whose individual members have been incorporated into the life of the white population through long coexistence. In many cases, they have not assimilated many manifestations of European culture. In others, they have substituted parts of this for their original civilization. This has resulted in an evolutionary cultural fusion in some cases and in an artificial, hybrid, and undesirable juxtaposition in others. The first case occurs when Indians gradually adopt new manifestations of culture by appropriating them to their own nature and necessities, or when they transform those of their own civilization by emptying them into new molds. In this case, fusion takes place with the wise intuition that comes with spontaneous evolution. The second case, what I have termed artificial, hybrid, and undesirable juxtaposition, has happened when the white race and invasive culture has sought to forcibly implant a new government, new habits, a new language, new needs . . . a new life breath! The Spanish monarchs understood that this was a terrible error and in order to avoid it, or at least to diminish its consequences, tried to expedite laws that favored the development of the indigenous race in preparation for its future incorporation. The Laws of the Indies can be seen as an effort in this direction. When this colonial legislation was abolished, the Indians from the groups represented by the Zapatistas of Morelos were once again neglected. The Laws of Reform favored those social elements of white race, mixed race, or even of people of pure Indian race whose civilization or culture was of European origin. The great Juarez, Indian by race but possessing a European culture, is a hero for the small part of the population whose conditions were improved by his laws and dispositions. But for the immense Indian or mixed majority, who holds the ideals of a distinct civilization, the figure of the great republican lacks significance.

"Why," one may ask, "is Juarez revered in all of the republic, if his value is limited to a small group within the population?" The answer is simple: that small minority of Mexicans has always had the voice and vote in our country. The aforementioned majority does not know how, is unable, or lacks the means with which to express its opinions. Ask those millions of creatures, Who is Juarez? They would not know how to answer, although the noble Zapotec effigy that appears in all municipal offices and government buildings would be familiar to most.

Given the lack of preparation of this indigenous majority, it is the persons of European civilization who must extend their hand to the Indian. It is our task to come to know the traditional spirit of their race, a race that faithfully guards all of its glories and sadnesses. We will see that even if these Indians do not commemorate specific personages as we do, they never forget the epochs of their painful past. They recall the picturesque pre-Hispanic life that disappeared over the centuries. They recall the spilling of blood during the Conquest and how the foresight of some Spanish rulers and missionaries was translated into legislation that was beneficial to them. And they recall that the newly independent republic, by throwing out these laws and formulating others, favored a small portion of the population and condemned indigenous people to abandonment. Since then, history has consisted of a long parade of rulers, each bringing new laws and antagonistic, artificial, and poorly suited systems of government. In a word, chaos. The dominant elements of the population have debated amongst themselves for a hundred years, whereas the indigenous people, the legitimate owners of the land, have been forced to live in passivity and servitude or died as canon fodder in disputes led by men of another race and with other ideas.

D. LET US CITE DIFFERENT EXAMPLES OF EVOLUTIONARY CULTURAL FUSION

1. *Economic Interests.* Indigenous groups of this third type have traditionally clung to the communal system in the pursuit of their material interests. Planting harvests, grazing and raising livestock, cutting down wood and fibers, and other productive tasks were conducted by indigenous communities that often united the functions of owner, exploiter, producer, seller, and consumer. It was a true system of mutualism that yielded such good results for the Indians that they came to prefer it. Of course, what has survived of these economic activities is not an unchanging reproduction of the society that flourished during the reign of Moctezuma or Ahuitzotl. Rather, these kinds of production have evolved, assimilating all of the most useful elements that European civilization had to offer. Tools and instruments, industrial and agricultural methods, commercial exchange, the transportation of products, proportional retribution of salaries, and the distribution of profits have all been adopted into their form of production. Overall, indigenous interests developed favorably under the communal system.

2. *Religion.* In the chapters titled "Our Religious Transition" and "Our Catholics," we discussed the religious beliefs of the groups that we referred to as "pagan Catholics," which we will build on here. Among these Indians, the village priest is a sacred and untouchable person. His saints are "more miraculous" than those of other villages; his churches are places privileged by divinity. His weddings, wakes, baptisms, and other ceremonies have a deep symbolism and elaborate ritual that includes both Catholic ideas and old pagan beliefs. Certain manifestations of external faith (the passion of Christ, the feast of Santiago, etc.) might appear ridiculous to modern sensibilities. However, these customs are venerable and sacred to these Indians and harmless to the larger national population.[2] Transforming them would be impossible, as Indians are generally characterized by the extreme suspicion with which they judge any intrusion into their religious world.

3. *Government.* In pre-Hispanic times, almost all of these Indian groups were ruled by patriarchal kings and pagan priests. During the Colonial period, the government of these creatures was left in the hands of encomenderos, soldiers, and Catholic missionaries. Only local governments remained in the charge of individuals who shared the Indians' blood, customs, and ideas. From the time of independence until today, the government of the regions in which these communities find themselves has gone from Pilate to Herod and from Herod to Pilate. In most cases, it was carried out by corrupt civilians and military men who belonged to a distinct race and brought with them distinct ideals. In other cases, the Indian caciques were even more harmful. Belonging to the same race as those they governed, they tortured them with greater intensity, being co-naturalized with their way of thinking. Their actions proved that saying, "there is no worse wedge than that made of the same wood."

E. REVISING PREVIOUS ATTEMPTS TO ACHIEVE ARTIFICIAL CULTURAL FUSION

1. *Interests.* Men were not created to mold themselves uniformly to laws—laws are made in accordance with the necessities of men. Since the different groups of our country present different necessities, it is logical that their laws should be different. The prohibition imposed on communal property and exploitation must be removed. What we are proposing does not constitute a

---

[2] The indigenous groups of North America and those of the English, German, and French colonies freely practice external faith.

retrograde tendency, because long experience has demonstrated the convenience that the communal system offers to the groups that we have discussed here. It is beneficial to them even if it is not appropriate to other groups that are more advanced or more primitive.

In this respect, the Laws of Reform[3] achieved a transcendent victory and suffered from a disastrous failure. The clergy—with few, but honorable, exceptions—had grabbed up enormous wealth and multiplied it through capable communal organization. It had grown so powerful that it constituted a true social danger. Because of this, the reformers worked together to decree the nationalization of those interests by prohibiting any and all communities from possessing goods or interests of any kind. This measure proved to be our salvation with regard to the clergy, and almost all countries that have been in a similar situation have followed the same course. But these same reform laws caused considerable harm to indigenous communities. Once the communal ownership of lands and the productive functions that this engendered were abolished, the territory held by indigenous communities became easy prey for large property holders who exploited the good faith and abused the disorientation, ignorance, and weakness of Indian communities.

2. *Religion*. No theologian, or any demolishing positivist, has been able to demonstrate who is more fanatical: if it is he who worships all gods or he who denies them all. Therefore, one must respect the Catholicism of these indigenous groups, however pagan it might appear to purists. Unfortunately, the Laws of Reform initiated the project of de-fanaticizing these groups. This was a useless and dangerous task, given that that fanaticism is now the same or greater than before. It is therefore essential that the current revolution develop a more ample and elevated liberalism from those of the past, so that we do not wound the religious sensibilities of those semi-pagan believers. The high clergy has also contributed to this problem, since they favor foreign priests and relegate the indigenous priests to a lesser status, a prejudice that instantly excites Indianist parishioners.

3. *Government*. If these groups fulfill their duties toward the federation and toward the state to which they belong, why not permit them to govern

---

[3] Referring to the Laws of Reform promulgated in the 1850s, which undermined certain privileges of the Catholic Church and the corporate landholdings of religious orders and indigenous communities.—Trans.

themselves with their own political systems and according to their own necessities, instead of imposing the systems of other national groups?

4. *The Proportion of These Groups*. These groups, typically represented by the population of the Zapatista region, doubtless make up from 30 to 40 percent of the total population of the country. Since they are currently passing through a stage of their evolution that groups like the Mayas and the Yaquis will inevitably pass through, there is an urgent need to study and resolve their problems. These problems relate to the fate of close to three quarters of our national population. Amongst the revolutionary proposals that have approached the Zapatista problem most sensibly, we must point out the work of General Pablo Gonzalez,[4] an intuitive and clairvoyant nationalist.

------

[4] Under the command of Venustiano Carranza, Pablo Gonzalez led the military defeat of Emiliano Zapata between 1916 and 1919 and established constitutionalist control in the Zapatistas' home state of Morelos. He ultimately orchestrated Zapata's assassination in 1919. Gonzalez later pledged allegiance to the "Sonoran Dynasty" after the assassination of Carranza in 1920 (see also the Introduction). —Trans.

Summary

The present moments are solemn.

The latest, the most intense of the revolutions that have moved the population of the republic for a century, tries to secure the conquest of national well-being. The others have failed in this attempt.

All Mexicans of good faith are authorized by their rights and obligated by their duty to collaborate in this most noble task in order to build the solid bases that in the future will sustain the durable and glorious work of national greatness.

The poorly ordered ideas presented in the previous pages were inspired by observations made regarding the majority of our population and interpreted by us defectively, but sincerely, as a humble contribution to our national resurgence.

Fusion of races, convergence and fusion of manifestations of culture, linguistic unification, and the economic equilibrium of social elements are concepts that are summarized in this book. They indicate conditions that must be established in the Mexican population, so that it may constitute and incarnate a powerful *patria* and a coherent and defined nationality.

Works Cited

Allen, John
    1989   Franz Boas' Physical Anthropology: The Critique of Racial Formalism Revisited. *Current Anthropology* 30(1): 79–84.

Armillas, Pedro
    1987   *La Aventura Intelectual de Pedro Armillas*, ed. José Luis de Rojas. Zamora, El Colegio de Michoacán.

Bartra, Roger
    1992   *The Cage of Melancholy: Identity and Metamorphosis in the Mexican Character*. New Brunswick, NJ, Rutgers University Press.
    2002a   *Blood, Ink and Culture: Miseries and Splendors of the Post-Mexican Condition*, trans. Mark Alan Healey. Durham, NC, Duke University Press.
    2002b   La Condición Post-Mexicana. In *La Anatomía del Mexicano*, ed. Roger Bartra, 303–310. Mexico, D.F., Plaza Janés.

Bernal, Ignacio
    1980   *A History of Mexican Archaeology: The Vanished Civilizations of Middle America*. New York, Thames and Hudson.

Bonfil Batalla, Guillermo
    1996   *México Profundo: Reclaiming a Civilization*. Austin, University of Texas Press.

Brading, David
    1973   *Los Orígenes del Nacionalismo Mexicano*. Mexico, D.F., Secretaría de Educación Pública.

Braun, Barbara

    1993   Diego Rivera's Collection: Art as Political and Artistic Legacy. In *Collecting the Pre-Colombian Past*, ed. Elizabeth Hill Boone, 251–270. Cambridge, MA, Harvard University Press.

Castañeda, Quetzil

    1996   *In the Museum of Maya Culture*. Minneapolis, University of Minnesota Press.

    2003   Stocking's Historiography of Influence: The "Story of Boas," Gamio and Redfield at the Cross-"Road to Light." *Critique of Anthropology* 23(3): 235–263.

Chuchiak, John F.

    1997   Intelectuales, los Indios y la Prensa, el Periodismo Polémico de Justo Sierra O'Reilly. *Saastun* 1(2): 3–49.

Cifuentes, Barbara

    2002   *Lenguas para un Pasado, Huellas de la Nación: Losa Estudios sobre Lenguas Indígenas en México en el Siglo XIX*. Mexico, D.F., INAH.

Comas, Juan

    1961   *Relaciones Inter-raciales en América Latina, 1940–1960*. Mexico, D.F., UNAM.

Córdova, Arnaldo

    1979a   *La Política de Masas y el Futuro de la Izquierda en México*. Mexico, D.F., Era.

    1979b   México: Revolución Burguesa y Política de Masas. In *Interpretaciones de la Revolución Mexicana*, ed. Adolfo Gilly, 55–90. Mexico, D.F., Nueva Imagen.

Davenport, Charles, and Morris Steggerda

    1929   *Race Crossing in Jamaica*. Washington, DC, Carnegie Institute of Washington.

de la Cadena, Beatriz

    2000   *Indigenous Mestizos: The Politics of Race and Culture in Cuzco, Peru, 1919–1991*. Durham, NC, Duke University Press.

de la Peña, Guillermo

    1996   Nacionales y Extranjeros en la Historia de la Antropología Mexicana. In *La Historia de la Antropología en Mexico*, ed. Metchthild Rutsch, 41–81. Mexico, D.F., Plaza y Valdez.

WORKS CITED

Errington, Shelly

1998   *The Death of Primitive Art and Other Tales of Progress.* Berkeley, University of California Press.

Florescano, Enrique

1993   The Creation of the Museo Nacional de Antropología of Mexico and Its Scientific, Educational and Political Purposes. In *Collecting the Pre-Columbian Past: A Symposium at Dumbarton Oaks 6th and 7th October 1990*, ed. Elizabeth Hill Boone, 81–104. Washington, DC, Dumbarton Oaks Research Library and Collection.

Gamio, Manuel

1909   Restos de la Cultura Tepaneca. *Anales del Museo Nacional de Antropología, Historia y Etnología* 1(6): 241–253.

1916   *Forjando Patria: Pro Nacionalismo.* Mexico, D.F., Porrua Hermanos.

1917   Investigaciones Arqueológicas en México. *Nineteenth International Congress of Americanists, Proceedings*, 125–133.

1922   *La Población del Valle de Teotihuacán, el Medio en Que se Ha Desarrollado; Su Evolución Étnica y Social; Iniciativas para Procurar su Mejoramiento, por la Dirección de Antropología, Siendo Director de las Investigaciones, Manuel Gamio.* Mexico, D.F., Departamento de Antropología.

1924   Sequence of Cultures in Mexico. *American Anthropologist* 26: 307–322.

1929   Dr. Gamio Fears Race Conflict. *Palacio* 33: 207–209.

1930   *Mexican Migration to the United Status: A Study in Human Migration and Adjustment.* Chicago, University of Chicago Press.

1931   *The Mexican Immigrant, His Life-Story.* Chicago, University of Chicago Press.

García Canclini, Nestor

1995   *Hybrid Cultures: Strategies for Entering and Leaving Modernity.* Minneapolis, University of Minnesota Press.

Gonzalez Gamio, Ángles

1987   *Manuel Gamio: Una Lucha sin Final.* Mexico, D.F., UNAM.

Hale, Charles

1989   *The Transformation of Liberalism in Late Nineteenth-Century Mexico.* Princeton, NJ, Princeton University Press.

Hewitt de Alcántara, Cynthia

1983   *Anthropological Perspectives on Rural Mexico.* Boston, Routledge and Kegan Paul.

WORKS CITED

Ivy, Marylin
  1995   *Discourses of the Vanishing: Modernity, Phantasm, Japan*. Chicago, University of Chicago Press.

Keen, Benjamín
  1971   *The Aztec Image in Western Thought*. New Brunswick, NJ, Rutgers University Press.

Krauz, Enrique
  1999   *Caudillos Culturales en la Revolución Mexicana*. Mexico, D.F., Tusquets.
  [1976]

Lomnitz, Claudio
  1989   *Exits from the Labyrinth*. Berkeley, University of California Press.
  1999   Barbarians at the Gate: A Few Remarks on the Politics of the "New Cultural History of México." *Hispanic American Historical Review* 79(2): 367–383.
  2001   *Deep Mexico, Silent Mexico*. Minneapolis, University of Minnesota Press.

Matos Moctezuma, Eduardo
  1979   Las Corrientes Arqueológicas en Mexico. *Nueva Antropología* 3(12): 7–25.
  1998   *Las Piedras Negadas: De la Coatlicue al Templo Mayor*. Mexico, D.F., Consejo Nacional para la Cultura y las Artes.

Miller, Marilyn Grace
  2004   *Rise and Fall of the Cosmic Race: The Cult of Mestizaje in Latin America*. Austin, University of Texas Press.

Mitchell, Timothy
  2002   *Rule of Experts: Egypt, Techno-Politics, Modernity*. Berkeley, University of California Press.

Molina Enriquez, Andrés
  1909   *Los Grandes Problemas Nacionales*. Mexico, D.F., Imprenta de A. Carranza.

Nahmad Sittón, Salomón, and Thomas Weaver
  1990   Manuel Gamio, el Primer Antropólogo Aplicado y su Relación con la Antropología Norteamericana. *América Indígena* 4: 291–322.

Nuttal, Zelia
  1910   The Island of Sacrificios. *American Anthropologist* 12: 257–295.

Ortiz, Fernando
  1995   *Cuban Counterpoint: Tobacco and Sugar*. Durham, NC, Duke University
  [1940] Press.

WORKS CITED

Patterson, Thomas
2001   *A Social History of Anthropology in the United States*. New York, Berg.

Provine, William B.
1973   Geneticists and the Biology of Race Crossing. *Science* 182(4114): 790–796.

Rama, Angel
1996   *The Lettered City*. Durham, NC, Duke University Press.

Ramos, Samuel
1934   *El Perfil del Hombre y la Cultura en México*. Mexico, D.F., Imprenta Mundial.

Rodríguez Garcia, Ignacio
1997   Recursos Ideológicos del Estado Mexicano: El Caso de la Arqueología. In *La Historia de la Antropología en México*, ed. Metchthild Rutsch, 83–115. Mexico, D.F., Plaza y Valdez.

Rosaldo, Renato
1989   *Culture and Truth: The Remaking of Social Analysis*. New York, Beacon.

Saez Pueyo, Carmen
2001   *Justo Sierra: Antecedentes del Partido Único en México*. Mexico, D.F., Porrua.

Sapir, Edward
1924   Culture, Genuine and Spurious. *American Journal of Sociology* 29(4): 401–429.

Semo, Enrique
1979   Reflexiones sobre la Revolución Mexicana. In *Interpretaciones de la Revolución Mexicana*, 135–150. Mexico, D.F., Nueva Imagen.

Shadle, Stanley
1994   *Andrés Molina Enríquez: Mexican Land Reformer of the Revolutionary Era*. Tucson, University of Arizona Press.

Sierra Mendez, Justo
1969   *The Political Evolution of the Mexican People*. Austin, University of Texas
[1902] Press.

Sierra O'Reilly, Justo
2002   Diario de Nuestro Viaje a los Estados Unidos. In *La Guerra de Castas*.
[1861] Mexico, D.F., CONACULTA.

WORKS CITED

Stern, Alexandra Minna

    1999   Buildings, Boundaries and Blood: Medicalization and Nation-Building on the Mexican Border, 1910–1930. *Hispanic American Historical Review* 79(1): 41–81.

Stocking, George

    1966   Franz Boas and the Concept of Culture in Historical Perspective. *American Anthropologist* 68(4): 867–882.

    1968   *Race, Culture and Evolution*. Chicago, University of Chicago Press.

Tenorio Trillo, Mauricio

    1995   *Mexico at the World's Fairs*. Berkeley, University of California Press.

    1999   Stereophonic Scientific Modernisms: Social Science between Mexico and the United States, 1880s–1930s. *The Journal of American History* 86(3): 1156–1187.

Tozzer, Alfred

    1933   Zelia Nuttal. *American Anthropologist* 35: 475–482.

Trigo, Abril

    2004   General Introduction. In *The Latin American Cultural Studies Reader*, ed. Ana del Sarto, Alicia Rios, and Abril Trigo, 1–13. Durham, NC, Duke University Press.

Vasconcelos, José

    1979   *La Raza Cósmica / The Cosmic Race*. Baltimore, Johns Hopkins University
    [1926] Press.

Vasquez León, Luis

    2003   *El Leviatán Arqueológico*. Mexico, D.F., CIESAS/Porrua.

Walsh, Casey

    2004   Eugenic Acculturation: Manuel Gamio, Migration Studies and the Anthropology of Development in Mexico, 1910–1940. *Latin American Perspectives* 138(31): 118–145.

Warman, Arturo

    1970   Todos Santos y Todos Difuntos: Crítica Histórica de la Antropología Mexicana. In *Eso Que Llaman la Antropología Mexicana*, ed. Arturo Warman, 9–38. Mexico, D.F., Nuestro Tiempo.

Womack, John

    1969   *Zapata and the Mexican Revolution*. New York, Knopf.

Zea, Leopoldo
   1945   *En Torno a una Filosofía Americana*. Mexico, D.F., Colegio de México.
   1953   *El Positivismo en México*. Mexico, D.F., Colegio de México.

Zerubavel, Yael
   1995   *Recovered Roots: Collective Memory and the Making of Israeli National Tradition*. Chicago, University of Chicago Press.

Index

Page numbers in italics indicate illustrations

www.ingramcontent.com/pod-product-compliance
Ingram Content Group UK Ltd.
Pitfield, Milton Keynes, MK11 3LW, UK
UKHW041842150726
7214IPUK00015B/110